For Julia,

i frei

P. ....

April 2010

Burma and Tudor History

The Life and Work of Charles Bayne
1860-1947

Nicholas Bayne

Edward Gaskell
DEVON

First published 2008
Edward Gaskell publishers
Old Sawmill
Grange Road
Bideford
Devon EX39 4AS

isbn   (10) 1 -898546 -94 -0
isbn   (13) 978 -1 -898546 -94 -8

© Nicholas Bayne

Burma and Tudor History

The Life and Work of Charles Bayne, 1860-1947

Nicholas Bayne

All rights reserved. No part of this publication may be reproduced, stored in a
retrieval system, or transmitted in any form by any means electronic, mechani-
cal, photocopying, scanning, recording or otherwise, without the prior written
permission of the publishers.

Typeset, printed and bound by
Lazarus Press
Caddsdown Business Park
Bideford
Devon
EX39 3DX
www.lazaruspress.com

Contents

List of Tables and Figures

List of Plates
(Between pages 64 and 65)

List of Principal Characters

Close Family

Charles Bayne	Indian Civil Service, Burma, and Tudor historian
Augusta Bayne	His wife, née Hodgkinson
Alice, Madge and Ronald Bayne	His children
Peter Bayne	His father
Rev Ronald Bayne	His elder brother
George James Spence Hodgkinson	His brother-in-law; Commissioner in Burma 1878-90; Judicial Commissioner, Mandalay 1890-1

ICS Colleagues in Burma

Sir Charles Bernard	Chief Commissioner of Burma 1880-3 and 1884-7
Sir Charles Crosthwaite	Chief Commissioner 1883-4 and 1887-90
Sir Frederic Fryer	Financial Commissioner 1888-91; Chief Commissioner and Lieutenant Governor 1895-1903
Frank Campbell Gates	Close junior colleague in the Secretariat 1887-99; Financial Commissioner 1907-1914
William Hall	Settlement officer, Henzada, 1884-6; Director for Agriculture 1888-90; Financial Commissioner 1902-7
Sir Alexander Mackenzie	Chief Commissioner 1891-2 and 1894-5
Sir George Scott	Active in the Shan States from 1886; Burma-China Boundary Commissioner 1898-1900

Donald Smeaton — Creator of land settlement regime; Chief Secretary 1887-8; Financial Commissioner 1891-1902

Sir Edward Symes — Secretary and Chief Secretary; Bayne's immediate superior 1885-7 and from 1891 till his death in 1901

Sir Herbert Thirkell White — Close colleague in Secretariat, as Secretary and Chief Secretary up to 1895; Lieutenant Governor, 1905-10

Academic Colleagues in Tudor History

Hugh Bellot — Professor of American History, London

William. H. Dunham — Professor of History, Yale University

Alan Gledhill — ICS Burma 1924-47; Professor of Oriental Laws, School of Oriental Studies (later SOAS)

H. Stuart Moore — Secretary of the Selden Society

Sir John Neale — Professor of History, University College, London

Alfred Pollard — Professor of Constitutional History, London

Theodore Plucknett — Professor of Legal History, London School of Economics, and Literary Director, Selden Society

Charles Bayne's Career in the Indian Civil Service (Burma)

Extracted from *Histories of Service*, Burma, with additional information in italics

Appointed after examination 1878
Arrived in Burma 27 December 1880
Assistant Commissioner, Henzada, January 1881
    Pyapon, September 1881
    Paungde, March 1882
Officiating Assistant Secretary, Rangoon, October 1883
Assistant Commissioner, Yandoon and Pantanaw, January 1884
    Myanaung, March 1884
    Paungde, January 1886
Junior Secretary to Chief Commissioner, April 1886
    (officiating from March 1886)
Under Secretary, April 1887
Officiating Secretary, August 1888
Deputy Commissioner, November 1888;
    continues as officiating Secretary
Marriage to Alice Augusta Hodgkinson, January 1890
Furlough from February 1890 to March 1891
Daughter Alice born February 1891
Confirmed as Secretary, March 1891
Officiating Chief Secretary, March-July, 1892
Revenue Secretary, March 1893
Daughter Margaret (Madge) born November 1893
Furlough from March 1895 to December 1896
Death of his father, Peter Bayne, February 1896
Son Ronald born August 1897
Member of Legislative Council, Burma, 1897,
    reappointed 1899 and 1901
Officiating Commissioner, Meiktila division, March-July 1898
Officiating Chief Secretary, Government of Burma, March 1899

Posted as officiating Commissioner, Minbu, June 1899,
    but recalled as Chief Secretary
Confirmed as Chief Secretary, January 1901,
    after death of Sir Edward Symes
Furlough from February to December 1901, *after breakdown*
Companion of the Star of India (CSI), November 1901
Attended Delhi Durbar, December 1902-January 1903
Furlough on medical certificate, August 1903 to August 1904
Commissioner, September 1903
Officiating Financial Commissioner and Member of Legislative
    Council, August 1904
Six months leave on private affairs, May 1906
Retired, November 1906

Preface

A century ago my grandfather left Burma at the end of his career in the Indian Civil Service (ICS). Charles Gerwien Bayne had arrived in Rangoon 25 years before, in December 1880. He rose to become Chief Secretary and Financial Commissioner of the provincial government, but still preferred to retire as soon as he could draw his pension. In his long retirement Charles Bayne devoted himself to research into English Tudor history. His first interest was in the early years of Queen Elizabeth I, on which he published three solid articles and a book up to 1913. Later he turned his interest to Henry VII, which led to another book, published after his death as the introduction to a collection of documents.

I am moved to reconstruct his life and achievements by more than family piety. Having spent my own professional life in the British Diplomatic Service, I feel a personal affinity with my grandfather's career as another overseas civil servant. I have found contemporary echoes in the Burma of his time. The third Burmese War of 1885 and the pacification that followed it have many parallels with the US-led occupation of Iraq from 2003 onwards. In the late 19th century the closed economy of Burma became exposed to international pressures very similar to the globalisation of today, leading to greater wealth but growing social tension.

I also find a strong sense of identity with my grandfather's retirement activities. Like him, I have turned to academic research after leaving the Diplomatic Service, though I have not reached the same high standard as he did. His work was based on meticulous analysis of original sources, including diplomatic correspondence of a kind with which I am very familiar. Because he left few personal papers, reconstructing his life requires the same sort of research in official documents that he himself practised.

Charles Bayne's professional career can be traced in the *Histories of Service* of ICS officers in Burma and in the Burma *Civil Lists* of the period, which are preserved in the India Office Records (see page viii above). I have filled out this skeleton from Burmese government reports, some of them signed C. G. Bayne, and official correspondence. More details come from the memoirs, private letters and diaries of others who served in Burma at the time, such as Sir Charles Crosthwaite (Chief Commissioner 1887-1890), Sir Frederic Fryer (Chief Commissioner and Lieutenant Governor 1895-1903), Donald Smeaton, Sir George Scott and Sir Herbert Thirkell White (Lieutenant Governor 1905-1910). Herbert White's memoirs, *A Civil Servant in Burma* (1913), are especially valuable for the first part of Charles Bayne's career, as they spent six years or more together in the Secretariat in Rangoon. Frederic Fryer's diary and the letters that he and his successor Sir Hugh Barnes exchanged with the Viceroys Lord Elgin and Lord Curzon are important for Bayne's later career.

The best sources for Charles Bayne's life and research in retirement are his published works themselves. These can be supplemented from the surviving correspondence that he conducted with various scholars about the publication of his last book. Hardly any of his other personal papers survive, apart from some legal documents, family photos and a few late letters. So I have had to resort to speculation about what he felt and what sort of person he was. I am emboldened to do this because, as his grandson, I feel able to attribute to him my own thoughts and reactions.

I am grateful for the help I have received from my brothers Christopher and David Bayne and my cousin Jane Rowley Williams, all, like me, grandchildren of Charles Bayne. I am indebted to my cousin Dominic Grieve, MP, for giving me access to the papers assembled by his late father, Percy Grieve, about the Hodgkinsons, my grandmother's family. I also express my thanks to Peter Lyon and Tim Shaw of the Institute of Commonwealth Studies, Vanessa West of the London School of Economics and Political Science and Barbara Wright of the Uppingham Association. A shorter account of Charles Bayne's Burmese career is published as 'Governing British Burma' in *The Round Table*, issue 389 (April 2007), thanks to the help and support of the Editor, Professor Andy Williams of the University of St Andrew's. Taylor & Francis, the publishers of the Journal, have kindly given me permission to re-use that material in the present work.

Finally, I am indebted to Anne Gowar of Bideford for introducing me to Lazarus Press. I am most grateful to Edward Gaskell for making my grandfather's biography into such a handsome and high quality book.

Nicholas Bayne
Hampton Court
August 2007

Lazarus Press

Chapter 1.

Ancestry, Birth and Education

The Bayne family originated in the far north of Scotland, when John Bane Mackay broke away from the main Clan Mackay after the battle of Drum-na-coup in 1431. Some of his descendants (by now called Bane or Bain) settled in Dingwall, a small town in Easter Ross, north-west of Inverness. Our earliest certain ancestor is the Rev Ronald Bayne, DD (1752-1821) – see family tree in Table 1.1. He was born in Dingwall and was probably descended both from the local lairds – the Baynes of Tulloch – and from the first Church of Scotland minister of the town, the Rev John Bayne (1686-1737), but the records are incomplete.

Ronald Bayne himself entered the Church of Scotland, after a turbulent youth when he was known as 'cursed Ronald'. He visited India, as chaplain to a Highland regiment, and ministered in Aberdeen and Kiltarlity, near Dingwall. He married Elizabeth Bentley, from a distinguished academic family. Her brother was a professor in Aberdeen and her great-uncle was Dr Richard Bentley, the famous classical scholar and Master of Trinity College Cambridge. This academic gene reappeared strongly in her descendants, especially my grandfather. The couple had five children and the youngest son, Charles John Bayne (1797-1832), followed his father into the Church of Scotland and became minister at Fodderty, just outside Dingwall. He married Isabella Duguid, also of an Aberdeen family. But Charles John died young, leaving his widow to bring up three young sons.

The second boy, Peter Bayne (1830-1896), was educated in Aberdeen and also intended to enter the Church of Scotland. But he had a weak chest, which meant he could not support the heavy preaching demands made on ministers. So he decided to become a writer and journalist instead. On taking his MA in 1850 he began writing for religious magazines in Edinburgh and in 1856 became editor of the evangelical paper the *Witness*, after the death of Hugh Miller, the Scottish geologist and church leader. He visited Germany to learn the language and met Clotilda Gerwien in Berlin. They were married in 1858 and their first son Ronald was born a year later.

In 1860 Peter Bayne left Edinburgh and moved to England – the first of his family to do so. He took up the post of editor of the *Dial* weekly newspaper, an ambitious new venture in London. He brought his family south and settled at 4 Gresham Road, Brixton, where his second son Charles, my grandfather, was born on 4 December 1860. The earliest photo of any Baynes shows Clotilda on a visit to Berlin in 1862, with her sons Ronald and Charles, aged 2 and 1 (Plate I).

But the *Dial* proved a financial failure and its collapse left Peter Bayne with heavy debts. In 1862 he left to become editor of the *Weekly Review*, the organ of the English Presbyterian Church. The Baynes' family increased by two daughters, Clotilda and Jane Isabella. But in 1865 Peter Bayne met another professional setback and a personal tragedy. He fell out with the Presbyterians over the inspiration of scripture and had to resign from the *Weekly Review*. His wife died in childbirth, leaving him with four small children to bring up. By now the family had moved out to Harlington, on the western fringes of London, and Clotilda is buried in the churchyard there.

From this low point Peter Bayne's fortunes revived and Charles seems to have had a happy childhood. His father soon married again and his second wife, Anna Mayo, proved a devoted stepmother. Charles and his siblings acquired lots of step-aunts and cousins. The family moved several times,

Table 1.1   **Family Tree of the Baynes**

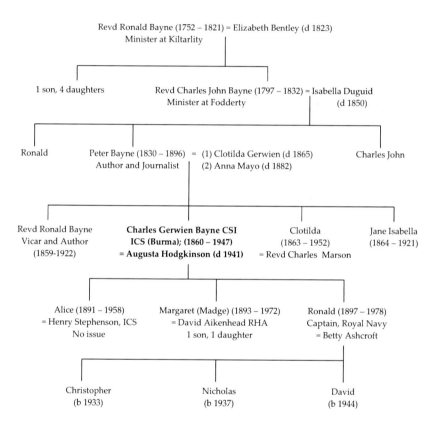

always staying in the suburbs: first to Worcester Park, Surrey, and later to Kilburn, nearer to Anna's relatives in Hampstead. Peter Bayne gave up editorial responsibilities but became a successful leader-writer for the *Christian World*. His published works moved away from strictly religious themes while Charles was growing up, to embrace biographies of Hugh Miller and Martin Luther, a play, a novel (under a pseudonym), a historical work on the Civil War and volumes of literary criticism. He also became closer to the Church of England: his elder son Ronald became an Anglican priest, while his daughter Clotilda married another. Charles would have absorbed from his father a love of writing and research and a strong sense of duty, all of which are evident in his later career.

In August 1874 Charles Bayne, aged 13, went to Uppingham School on a scholarship. Uppingham was then in its great period of growth under its famous headmaster, Edward Thring. But in July 1877 Peter Bayne took his son away from the school, evidently to give him a year's 'cramming' for the entrance exam for the India Civil Service (ICS) in the following year. The Baynes had no direct links with India, since the Rev Ronald's brief visit 80 years before, and there are no signs that his second wife, Anna Mayo, had Indian connexions either. (The Earl of Mayo had been a respected Governor-General from 1868 to 1872, but this is a coincidence; the family name was Bourke, not Mayo.)

But Peter Bayne no doubt heard about the ICS from the ecclesiastical circles that he frequented, because clergymen's sons provided a quarter of new entrants. After the many setbacks in his own career in writing and journalism, he may well have advised his younger son to choose the ICS as a more settled profession. The ICS certainly provided a predictable career structure, with regular promotion, generous pay and a guaranteed pension of £1000 a year after 25 years service. ICS officers had to spend their working lives in unhealthy conditions far from Britain. But they could take long home leave, called 'furlough', for up to two years after eight years of service and thereafter at four-yearly intervals.

Charles Bayne successfully sat the ICS exam in the summer of 1878. In most years there were about 200 ICS candidates, of whom 40 or so were taken. Under the reforms just being introduced by Lord Salisbury, as Secretary of State for India, new entrants to the ICS were then sent to university for two years to complete their probation. Charles Bayne went to University College, Oxford, where he joined his elder brother Ronald and also met Charles Marson, who would later marry his sister Clotilda. As an ICS probationer, Charles Bayne was set to study law (with visits to courts to attend trials), as well as the history, language and administration of the part of India to which he was assigned. He was allocated at first to Bengal, which took the largest number of new entrants. During his probation he studied Bengali, being awarded £15 for his proficiency.

At the end of his probation he passed his confirmation exam and received his certificate of entry to the ICS in August 1880. This stated that 'in respect of seniority Charles Gerwien Bayne is entitled to the first place among the selected candidates for the Bengal Division'. A further certificate signed by the Under-Secretary for India instructed him to take the P & O liner sailing on 10 November to Calcutta 'and there report himself to the Secretary of Government'. Charles Bayne parted from his family, whom he could not expect to see for several years, and took the boat from Southampton through the Suez Canal.

Up to this point Charles Bayne probably expected a career in Bengal. The surviving documents make no mention of Burma. At this time Burma was administered by ICS members from the Bengal service; it only began recruiting its own civil servants – the Burma Commission – from 1881. Few ICS candidates volunteered for Burma, however, because of its unhealthy climate. At a late stage therefore, possibly only on his arrival in Calcutta, Charles Bayne was re-assigned to fill a vacancy in Burma. On 27 December, shortly after his 20th birthday, he finally reached Rangoon, to begin a new life.

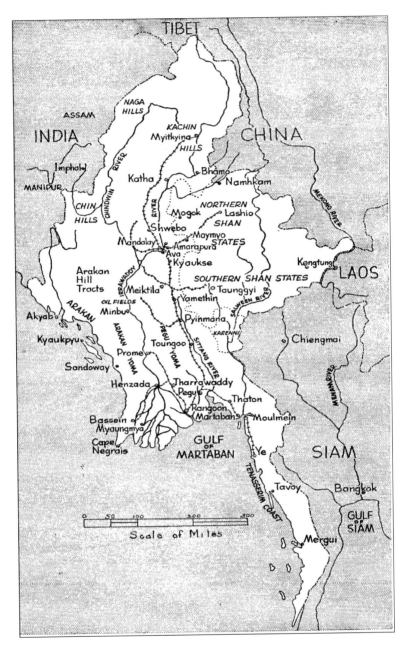

Map of Burma

Chapter 2

In the Districts of Lower Burma

On the map Burma, then as now, looked like an old-fashioned kite with a tail (see previous page). The main part of the country was a diamond, 900 miles (1500 km) north to south and 600 miles (1000 km) east to west and enclosed on all four sides by mountains. It bordered Siam (now Thailand) on the south-east, China on the north-east and India on the north-west, while its south-western limit, beyond the Arakan mountains, was formed by the Bay of Bengal. The great Irrawaddy river divided the country from north to south, creating a wide delta where it flowed into the sea. Other rivers flowed parallel to it: the Chindwin to the west, the Sittang and the Salween to the east.

The Burmans proper lived in the central river valleys and their capital cities, Pagan, Ava, Amarapura and later Mandalay, were near the centre of the diamond. The mountainous frontier districts were occupied by other peoples – Shans to the east, Kachins to the north and Chins to the north-west. These hill tribes attracted a lot of interest from anthropologists and other writers, but since Charles Bayne never visited them we can ignore them.

The Kingdom of Burma had a history going back to the 11th century, when the dynasty founded by King Anawratha established itself at Pagan. Successive kings covered the plain beside the Irrawaddy with Buddhist shrines and temples, which remain to this day. But this early kingdom collapsed as a result of Mongol raids over the Chinese border at the time of Kublai Khan and several centuries of confusion followed. In the 16th century the Toungoo dynasty regained control over the entire country again and fixed their capital at Ava. The Burmese kings looked inland, defending their frontier with China and waging several wars against Siam. They took little interest in the Portuguese, French and British traders establishing themselves along the coast.

All this changed after King Alaungpaya founded the Konbaung dynasty in the 1750s. He and his successors adopted a much more expansionist policy, after overcoming Siam and defeating incursions from China. King Bodawpaya (ruled 1782-1819) conquered the coastal district of Arakan, which for the first time brought the Kingdom of Burma into direct – and fatal – contact with British India. After a generation of raids across the border, the next Konbaung king, Bagyidaw (1819-1837), sent his general Bandula to occupy Assam and attempt a pre-emptive strike against Bengal. This provoked the first Burmese war of 1824-1826. By the treaty of Yandabo Britain obliged the Burmese to cede Arakan and Tenasserim, narrow strips of coastline on the Bay of Bengal, including the tail of Burma's kite.

Arakan and Tenasserim each became divisions in the charge of a Commissioner, but Rangoon, the main port, remained in the hands of the king of Burma. A dispute there between British naval captains and the local governor provoked Lord Dalhousie, the Viceroy in Calcutta, to launch the second Burmese war in 1852. After a brisk campaign, Britain annexed Rangoon and the territory going about 200 miles up the Irrawaddy river, which became the division of Pegu. Ten years later the three divisions were combined into the single province of British Burma, under a Chief Commissioner at Rangoon, which became the colonial capital. All the hinterland was ruled, directly or indirectly, by King Mindon (1853-1878) from his capital Mandalay.

British Burma was administered in the same way as other provinces of India. Each division was divided into about five districts in the charge of Deputy Commissioners. These were the leading executive officers in Burma, responsible for justice, law and order and tax collection in their districts. As in Indian frontier provinces they were drawn equally from the ICS and the British Army. On arrival in Burma, new ICS entrants became Assistant Commissioners and were assigned to a district. They could expect to spend five to ten years as Assistant Commissioners in the field, gradually gaining more responsibility. Because of absences through leave and sickness, they would often be called upon to 'officiate' for their superiors.

The expatriate colonial administrators of the Burma Commission were superimposed on the regime that had prevailed under the Kingdom of Burma. This had its own hierarchy. Traditionally, members of the royal family and leading courtiers would be allocated revenues from rural communities, from which they gained their titles. A Burmese prince or courtier might be called the *myoza* (literally the 'eater') of Moulmein, for example, which was the source of his income, though he would have no governing function there. More recently, the Konbaung kings had sent out their own provincial administrators, called *myowuns*, whose authority came from the capital.

At local level, however, justice, law and order and tax collection had been in the hands of a hereditary magnate, the *myothugyi*, who controlled a township or a 'circle' of villages. These *thugyis* were trusted and respected in their community, while the *myozas* and *myowuns* were feared and avoided whenever possible. When the British took over in Lower Burma they replaced the *myowun* with the *myook*, or township officer, who took orders from the Deputy Commissioner. They organised their own courts and police force. They retained the *thugyi*, but merely as a revenue collector, while law and order at local level was entrusted to inferior officials.

Early Posts in the Irrawaddy Valley

Charles Bayne was the only ICS entrant assigned to Burma in 1880. During his first few days in Rangoon he would have met the Chief Commissioner and the Commissioner of his first division – both remote Olympian figures for a new arrival, but they would be highly influential in his later career. Charles Bernard, the Chief Commissioner, had been officiating in Rangoon from 1880 and was confirmed in the appointment two years later. Though it was his first time in Burma, he soon developed an excellent understanding of the local peoples. He was an immensely hard-working man with a prodigious memory, though he found it hard to delegate. George Hodgkinson, the Commissioner, was about to take over the new Irrawaddy division, carved out of populous Pegu. He had recently come to Burma seeking promotion after a career in Bengal. He was not only an able administrator but remarkable for his family loyalty. Though unmarried himself, he invited four of his sisters in turn to live with him and found husbands for them all. As a later chapter will tell, Charles Bayne would marry the youngest, Alice Augusta Hodgkinson.

Without delay Charles Bayne was appointed a magistrate of the third class and despatched on 9 January 1881 to Henzada, his first posting. Henzada was the northernmost district of the new Irrawaddy division, stretching along the West bank of the river about 75 miles (120 km) north-west of Rangoon. Apart from the foothills of the Arakan mountains to the west, the district was all flat plain and would originally have been only sparsely populated, because the river Irrawaddy regularly submerged it in time of flood. But over a ten-year campaign, up to 1872, the Public Works Department of the provincial government had created great embankments, which prevented flooding and made all the land available for growing rice. The population of Henzada district had therefore grown rapidly and rice production had expanded. The surplus was exported not only to India but also to Europe once the Suez Canal opened in 1869.

Charles Bayne would have found the scenery 'generally dull and uninteresting – unending vistas of rice-fields and swamps on one drab level', the climate not excessively hot but 'damp, dull and depressing' and the local population easy-going, cheerful and hospitable, though prone to outbreaks of anger – all according to the *Burma Gazetteer*. Henzada town, the district headquarters, was a settlement of some 16,000 inhabitants and one of Burma's earliest municipalities, with its own municipal school and hospital. Charles Bayne would have been based there, working under the guidance of Major Horace Spearman, the Deputy Commissioner. He was put in charge of the Treasury, learnt how to try simple legal cases and often accompanied the Deputy Commissioner on tour. At the same time he studied for the exams, in law, financial management and the Burmese language, that he was expected to pass in his first two years. Herbert Thirkell White, who had reached Burma three years ahead of Charles Bayne, followed the same routine. White confesses in his memoirs, *A Civil Servant in Burma*: 'I had a charmingly idle time'. Charles Bayne was probably more studious and serious-minded.

After nine months at Henzada, Charles Bayne moved to the other end of Irrawaddy division and was put in charge of Pyapon, a sub-division of Thonegwa district, from September 1881. Pyapon was right down at the seaward edge of the Irrawaddy delta, close to Rangoon. It was surrounded by tidal creeks and waterways, which swarmed with crocodiles, and much of the area was submerged during the monsoon. The climate was even more humid than Henzada, with 95 inches (240 cm) of rain a year, but was cooler because of sea-breezes. Though infested with mosquitoes, the district was not reckoned to be unhealthy. Rice was grown on the land above the water-level, but the main economic activity was fishing and especially preparing the evil-smelling fish sauce called *ngapi* much loved by the Burmese.

Charles Bayne was now appointed magistrate of the second class and became responsible for his own sub-division. His

Deputy Commissioner, Frank Copplestone, was based at Maubin, some 40 miles to the north. Like Herbert White, who had been in charge of Pantanaw in the same district, Charles Bayne would have been his own township officer at Pyapon. He would have tried all civil and criminal cases, copied English correspondence and done all the revenue and executive work of the township. He would have found time to be on tour about half of every month, always travelling by water, and would have every incentive to practice his Burmese. He stayed six months in Pyapon; then, in March 1882, following usual custom, he was posted to a different division. He moved back up the Irrawaddy river to Paungde, a sub-division of Prome district. Prome was part of Pegu division; Colonel Charles Walker was the Commissioner and Major George Alexander the Deputy Commissioner.

The city of Prome had been the site of the earliest recorded civilisation in Burma, the Pyus, dating to around 500 AD. Its main importance in the 1880s was as the northern terminus of the first railway to be built in Burma. Passengers from Rangoon would take the train to Prome and there transfer into river steamers, to continue their journey up the Irrawaddy to Mandalay and Upper Burma. Charles Bayne's sub-division stretched along the east bank of the Irrawaddy and the climate was hotter than he had yet known. But there was still 55 inches (135 cm) of annual rainfall, which made it one of the main rice-growing areas of the district. The sub-division also included the Inma lake, with a thriving fishery, and some teak forests in the foothills of the Pegu mountains. Paungde town, 32 miles (50km) from Prome and 130 miles (200 km) from Rangoon, was a station on the railway. It had about 10,000 inhabitants, a hospital and a middle school and was the site of the provincial reformatory.

Charles Bayne stayed in Paungde for eighteen months. He continued to try legal cases, to oversee revenue collection and to tour the outlying villages of his sub-division, by horseback or bullock-cart. He was also able to complete his professional studies. In June 1882 he passed his Higher Standard exams in Treasury and Local Fund Accounts, Revenue and Law and at once became magistrate, first class. At that time he also passed Burmese Lower Standard and achieved Burmese Higher Standard the following year, just as he was being posted to Rangoon. Throughout his career he clearly kept his Burmese language skills at a high level, since he acted as examiner in Burmese for the ICS entry after his retirement.

Land Settlement and Tax Collection
From early October 1883 Charles Bayne was attached to the Secretariat in Rangoon for four months. This short posting proved the most important of his early years and will be covered in the next chapter. On leaving Rangoon at the end of January 1884, Charles Bayne spent six weeks looking after two adjacent sub-divisions in the delta, Yandoon and Pantanaw, not far from his early haunt of Pyapon. In March he went back to Henzada district, and stayed for nearly two years; Captain James Butler was now the Deputy Commissioner, while George Hodgkinson was still Commissioner. Bayne became the sub-divisional officer in charge at Myanaung, the next major town upstream from Henzada, about 50 miles (80 km) to the north and just across the river from Paungde. Myanaung town had 7,000 inhabitants and was made a municipality while he was there. It was still in the flat, rice-growing plain of the Irrawaddy, though this was less fertile than further south, as there was less rainfall. The area was unhealthy because of the difficulty of getting reliable supplies of clean water and Charles Bayne had to cope with a serious cholera epidemic during his posting.

He would also have assisted in the first British land settlement of the district, which was carried out by William Hall as settlement officer. The purpose of the settlement was to establish the agricultural capacity of the land and, on that basis, to fix the assessment for land tax, which was the main source of revenue for the province. After a detailed cadastral survey of the holdings, the settlement officer would estimate all the circumstances that would affect the value of the crop – size of holding, type of soil, annual rainfall and so forth. All these details were entered in the settlement report ('as in a Domesday Book' says the *Burma Handbook*) and provided the assessment on which each cultivator would pay his taxes annually. Later in his career Charles Bayne would be much concerned with land revenue and William Hall would again be a close colleague. In 1884-5, however, his direct responsibility was to oversee the collection of revenue for his sub-division, which he did well. In the report on revenue administration for Irrawaddy division that he submitted to Rangoon, George Hodgkinson wrote: 'Special commendation is due to C. G. Bayne, Assistant Commissioner Myanaung'.

From June to August 1885 Charles Bayne had his first spell of privilege leave since reaching Burma. ICS officers earned one month's leave a year. But they could accumulate up to three months to be taken together, which would just give them time to get back to Britain, at the cost of spending up to half their leave at sea. Charles Bayne may well have taken advantage of this, especially to see his father again and to visit the grave, in Harlington churchyard, of his beloved stepmother Anna Mayo, who had died in 1882. His friend Herbert White, whom he had got to know in Rangoon, escaped from the Secretariat to take over the sub-division of Myanaung in his absence. Both men were due for new postings; but when Bayne got back from his leave he found White had been recalled to Rangoon. Tension was mounting with the Kingdom of Burma. In November 1885 the third Burmese war broke out. Charles Bayne at Myanaung would have watched the British flotilla sail north to attack Mandalay and wondered what this would mean for him. For the moment he stayed on in Myanaung till the end of the year and then moved across the river to resume his old post at Paungde, on the railway. But this was to be a temporary assignment; he was being held in reserve for more important work in Rangoon.

ICS officers paint an Arcadian picture of life in the districts of Lower Burma at this time. It was very different from the rest of India. The climate was hot and humid, but never reached the extreme temperatures of the Indian plains. The country was fertile, green and lush, well watered by the great rivers and the monsoon rains, and drought was unknown. The people earned a comfortable living from rice farming, which gave them enough surplus to be hospitable and charitable and enough leisure to enjoy plays and dancing. There were no religious tensions or taboos. Buddhism was the most tolerant of religions and the monasteries in every village provided elementary education for boys, so that most Burmese men were literate and a proportion of women too. Burmese women had great freedom, for example to own property or divorce their husbands, and moved easily in society at all levels. Many ICS officers cohabited with Burmese women – more than 90 per cent, according to one source; we do not know if Charles Bayne was among them. When challenged to mend his ways, an officer would often prefer to marry his mistress than reject her; one Deputy Commissioner even conducted his own wedding service.

Charles Bayne would have enjoyed these idyllic delights during his first five years, but he turned his back on them. By now he had gained a wide experience of judicial, revenue, finance and general administration at district level. Many of his colleagues preferred to continue with judicial work, which would keep them in the districts. But although Charles Bayne became deeply interested in the law in his retirement, he did not pursue it in Burma. He had been commended for his work in land and revenue administration, which required perseverance and meticulous attention to detail. These were the talents most prized in the Secretariat in Rangoon, where he would spend the rest of his career.

Table 3.1.   The Government of British (Lower) Burma, October 1883

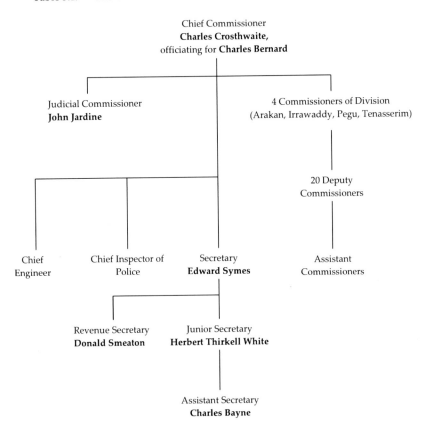

Chapter 3

The Secretariat in Peace and War

When Charles Bayne went to Rangoon in October 1883 for his short spell in the Secretariat, Charles Bernard was on leave. The officiating Chief Commissioner was Charles Crosthwaite, a forceful, decisive, even ruthless man, who would succeed Bernard from 1887 to 1890. In this first spell in the Secretariat Charles Bayne met three men who would become his closest colleagues in the years ahead. As a group of four they would dominate the central administration of Burma, under successive Chief Commissioners, for the next two decades. The first was Edward Symes, described as 'one of the most brilliant men of his time'. But he never married and was eventually worn down by the pressure of work, so that his career came to a tragic end. The second was Donald Smeaton, an able but opinionated Scot, who liked to challenge the conventional wisdom. But he did this too often, so his career ended in disappointment. The third was Herbert Thirkell White, who emerges from his memoirs as a good-humoured, enterprising, self-confident man with strong common sense. 'Altogether,' says White, 'I spent in the office [the Secretariat] eleven years, a period surpassed only by my friend Mr C. G. Bayne'. As compared with the others, Charles Bayne appears less brilliant and extrovert. But he held his own as the fourth member of the quartet thanks to a methodical mind, a gift for financial administration and a great capacity for expressing himself on paper.

In October 1883 the central government of British Burma was extremely small (see Table 3.1). The Chief Commissioner was the head of the provincial government, but he had no independent power of legislation. All laws and regulations for Burma were adopted by the Government of India in Calcutta, though they might be drafted in Rangoon. He was supported by a Judicial Commissioner who was the supreme legal authority, except in Rangoon itself, where there was a Recorder. His Secretariat consisted of the Secretary, who was Edward Symes, officiating for George Burgess; the Junior Secretary, who was Herbert White; and the Assistant Secretary, who was Charles Bayne. The office was completed by a number of British and Burmese clerks. The task of the Secretariat was to process the instructions received from the Government of India in Calcutta and to spread them round to the more numerous administrators in the districts. It prepared the Chief Commissioner's correspondence and drafted the many reports required by Calcutta. These were issued in final form by the government printer in Rangoon as 'Blue Books' – folio volumes bound in blue paper covers. The Secretariat also drew up the province's budget and centralised all the tax revenue, remitting to Calcutta the required surplus that was used to fund central Indian expenditure, especially on the army.

Donald Smeaton was in Rangoon on a special assignment. He had come to Burma from the North-West Provinces in 1879 to organise the system of land and revenue administration. The land settlement conducted by William Hall, helped by Charles Bayne, in Henzada district, was one of the first carried out under Smeaton's new system. Donald Smeaton now held the posts of Revenue and Settlement Secretary and Director for Agriculture, though these lapsed after his departure in 1884. The headquarters team was completed by the Chief Inspector of Police and the Chief Engineer. The latter was head of the Public Works Department, which was much concerned with building a second railway line northwards towards Mandalay up the Sittang valley; this reached the border of British Burma by 1885.

In 1883, says Herbert White, 'the work in the Secretariat was hard enough, but not as overwhelming as in later times'. Charles Bayne, who first appears in White's book at this point, was officiating as Assistant Secretary while the regular incumbent was on privilege leave. He would have helped to prepare the annual Administration Report and see through the press the Departmental Reports and Resolutions, as White himself had done three years before. A major preoccupation in the whole of India at this time was the Ilbert Bill, introduced by the Legal Member of the Viceroy's Council. The bill was intended to give powers to native Indian judges to try British and other European residents. This was bitterly resisted by non-official British opinion in India, so that the provisions were heavily watered down before adoption. Resistance took time to gather force in remote Burma, but a protest meeting was eventually planned in Rangoon, just as news of the dilution of the law reached the Secretariat. They decided to deflate the opposition by planting a parody of the proceedings at the meeting in advance in the *Rangoon Gazette*. As White tells the story: 'The plot was hatched in the Secretariat. Though I was *pars exigua* [a very small part], the account was mainly written by Mr Bayne. The secret was never disclosed.' The story shows Charles Bayne had a ready pen, a lively sense of humour and sufficient confidence to be part of such an enterprise.

Charles Bayne left the Secretariat in late January 1884, having shown aptitude for the work. Smeaton went back to the North-West Province of India. Sir Charles Bernard returned from leave and became increasingly preoccupied by relations with Upper Burma.

Causes of the Third Burmese War
King Mindon, who had taken the throne in 1853 after the second Burmese War, had been a strong and imaginative ruler. From his new capital at Mandalay he had tried to modernise

his traditional kingdom. He replaced his royal council by a cabinet of ministers, with specific responsibilities, and created a paid civil service to support them. But this inevitably created some administrative confusion, while the economic resources of the kingdom were inadequate to finance the reforms. The Burmese kings had earlier used international trade as a source of wealth. But the British now controlled Burma's main access to the outside world and contrived to siphon off the profits from trade. Commercial links with China, the only alternative outlet, were frustrated by rebellion in the frontier provinces. For these and other reasons, relations with Britain became strained. The Indian Government in Calcutta would have liked to treat Upper Burma like other native states, under the guidance of a British Resident. But Mindon and his court wanted to assert Burma's independent sovereignty. A Burmese embassy to London was pleased to be received by Queen Victoria, but shocked that she was supported by the Secretary for India, not the Foreign Secretary.

Mindon had died in 1878, shortly before Charles Bayne's arrival. His reforms were still insecure and he had not named an heir. His ministers wanted a pliable king, who would give them a free hand. They joined forces with the ambitious senior queen, who wanted to retain power but had no sons, only three daughters. Thibaw, the son of a junior queen (Mindon had fifty-three wives and concubines altogether) was in love with Supayalat, the middle princess; they were rapidly married and Thibaw was put onto the throne. But the modernising hopes of the ministers were soon disappointed. Supayalat, if not Thibaw, wanted to exercise personal power. Most of the rest of the royal family were soon massacred, to secure Thibaw's position on the throne. This nearly led to British intervention in 1879, but Calcutta was distracted by a crisis in Afghanistan and London by the Zulu War.

During the early 1880s the extravagance of Thibaw's court and the confusion persisting from Mindon's reforms caused a gradual breakdown of royal authority throughout Upper

Burma, while tension with Britain persisted. Thibaw's advisers tried to gain economic support and to promote Burmese independence by links with other European powers. They found a ready response from France, which aspired to expand its colonies in Indo-China. A new French Consul, who reached Mandalay in 1885, offered Thibaw the prospect of arms supplies, a French bank to ease his financial problems, new railway links and other commercial advantages. This emboldened Thibaw to have his Council impose a punitive fine on the British company exploiting the teak forests of Upper Burma, for alleged under-payment of taxes and royalties.

The British authorities, in Rangoon, Calcutta and London, could not tolerate the French encroachment into Burma, even though Paris disowned its Consul in Mandalay. They also protested vigorously at the fine imposed on the Bombay-Burma Trading Corporation. Business circles in Rangoon and Britain clamoured for Thibaw to be deposed and Upper Burma to be annexed to the British Empire, believing – quite wrongly – that this would open up a rich trade with China. Sir Charles Bernard was strongly opposed to annexation. He knew that though the Burmese hated Thibaw they were attached to the monarchy. He foresaw great difficulty in establishing control over Upper Burma. The Viceroy in Calcutta, Lord Dufferin, was hesitant; but the British government, headed by Lord Salisbury, insisted on action. Dufferin decided that, if Thibaw would not cooperate, there was no alternative to annexation and Bernard reluctantly agreed. In November 1885 he sent an ultimatum to Thibaw: he must submit the timber dispute to arbitration, accept a British resident and admit British oversight over his foreign policy. When Thibaw rejected the ultimatum, a British invading force sailed up the Irrawaddy, meeting very little resistance. Thibaw and Supayalat were easily removed from Mandalay and sent into exile in India.

'The country was taken and its government destroyed before we had decided what we should do with it, or considered the effect on the people,' wrote Sir Charles Crosthwaite, Bernard's successor as Chief Commissioner. Bernard favoured preserving the monarchy, but this proved impracticable. Only two suitable princes had survived Thibaw's massacre, of whom one had died earlier in 1885 and the other had fallen under the control of France. So a brief proclamation on 1 January 1886, in London and Calcutta, annexed Upper Burma to the Queen-Empress's dominions. Lord Dufferin, the Viceroy of India, then visited Mandalay and held long conferences there with Bernard and his staff, who included Herbert White. As a result, the Viceroy issued an order that from 1 March 1886 Upper Burma should be combined with Lower Burma to become a province of British India.

'The Mandalay campaign was undertaken with a light heart, in the belief that the people of Upper Burma would welcome us with open arms', wrote Donald Smeaton in *The Loyal Karens of Burma*, published in 1887. 'Events have proved how ill-founded this belief was.' The Burmese bitterly opposed the abolition of the monarchy, as being the symbol of national unity and sponsor of the Buddhist church. Thibaw's army scattered all over Upper Burma to provide the focus for widespread rebellion. The 10,000 British and Indian troops of the initial invading force soon proved inadequate to subdue the country and their numbers were doubled by the end of the year. The total forces engaged eventually reached over 30,000, including military police, and restoring order to Upper Burma occupied the rest of the decade. Kipling (who had wanted to cover the campaign) wrote about the fighting in Burma with a combination of broad comedy and harsh brutality. In his story 'The Taking of Lungtungpen' a party of English recruits capture a Burmese village stark naked. His poem 'The Grave of a Hundred Head' has an Indian platoon avenge the death of their English subaltern by killing a hundred Burmese and piling their heads on his tomb.

Promotion and Moving to Rangoon

The annexation had more than doubled the size of British Burma, which required a complete overhaul of the administration of the province. During 1886 four new divisions were created in Upper Burma and administrators – both ICS men and soldiers – had to be found to staff them, many being brought in from other parts of India. The Burma Commission was doubled in size, from 60 to 120 officers. The problems of Upper Burma kept Sir Charles Bernard in Mandalay. As soon as Lord Dufferin's decision took effect, on 1 March 1886, he created a separate Upper Burma Secretariat, headed by Herbert White. To look after Lower Burma in his absence, Bernard appointed a Special Commissioner in Rangoon and chose George Hodgkinson for the post. Edward Symes was confirmed as Secretary. Charles Bayne was called back to Rangoon to support Hodgkinson and Symes and must have caught the first available train from Paungde. As early as 2 March he began as officiating Junior Secretary and he was confirmed in the post on 1 April.

Charles Bayne evidently owed his appointment from having impressed George Hodgkinson with his work in Irrawaddy division. Edward Symes must also have thought well of his performance as Assistant Secretary, three years before, to accept him as Junior Secretary. Now aged 26, he thus received his first substantive promotion and began an uninterrupted spell of 17 years in the Secretariat. In his work over the next twelve months he would have been in daily contact with both George Hodgkinson and Edward Symes, who became friends as well as colleagues. He had less opportunity to impress Sir Charles Bernard, who was rarely in Rangoon and does not mention him in his surviving letters.

The Rangoon Secretariat had to run Lower Burma and keep supplies and men moving north to support the operations there. But the first task was to counter uprisings in Lower Burma, which had been provoked by the overthrow of the monarchy. 'Insurrection broke out all over the country', wrote

Herbert White, 'For a time Lower Burma was a seething mass of disorder'. A gang of rebels murdered a Deputy Commissioner in the Irrawaddy delta and then moved up-river to terrorise Charles Bayne's old district of Henzada. Everywhere the local police proved totally unable to deal with the outbreaks and the military had to be brought in. During the year order was gradually restored throughout Lower Burma, though this required another 7,000 troops. The Karens, a minority people scattered throughout the country, also proved loyal and helped to put down uprisings. But the Rangoon Secretariat resisted pressure to arm the Karens against the Burmese, fearing that this would only make matters worse. Donald Smeaton quotes at length in *The Loyal Karens of Burma* from urgent and sometimes intemperate letters from Dr Vinton, an American missionary to the Karens. Vinton fulminates against an unnamed Secretariat official who refused to issue him guns. This must have been Charles Bayne, as Vinton would have known Symes.

Meanwhile, Sir Charles Bernard, 'single-handed, organised and directed the administration of the new province, doing the work of three ordinary men'. But, says White, 'the effort was beyond even those exceptional powers'. He had wanted to rebuild civil government in Upper Burma on the foundations of the existing regime, but the chaos left by Thibaw's reign frustrated his aim. The heavy responsibilities put a severe strain on his health and he had to leave Burma early in March 1887. Because of his initial resistance to the annexation he was not offered another post in India and he went back to London to head a department in the India Office. The energetic Sir Charles Crosthwaite took over as Chief Commissioner.

Chapter 4

Pacifying Burma under Crosthwaite

From the start Sir Charles Crosthwaite disliked the division of the two Secretariats, where only Bernard had known what was happening in both parts of the province. In April 1887, soon after his arrival, he was given some extra resources for the Secretariat and took the opportunity to reorganise it on a more unified basis, bringing together the group that had worked for him in 1883. Though he praised George Hodgkinson, who was made Companion of the Star of India (CSI), he suppressed his post of Special Commissioner and despatched him to be Commissioner in Tenasserim, the southernmost division of Burma. He confirmed Edward Symes in the new post of Chief Secretary but immediately sent him off on well-earned furlough, recalling Donald Smeaton to officiate for him. The Upper Burma Secretariat was wound up and Herbert White was called down to Rangoon to become the Secretary. Charles Bayne was confirmed as the Under Secretary, also a new post. Frank Campbell Gates was made the Junior Secretary and, like the original quartet, would become a long-serving member of the Secretariat from now on.

Crosthwaite clearly liked and trusted Herbert White and Charles Bayne. He used them as a team and they worked very closely together. When White was delayed in Mandalay, Crosthwaite wrote to him in May 1887: 'Bayne has ably represented you'. He ended a letter to him in December: 'Wishing you a Happy New Year and the same to Bayne'. Several of Crosthwaite's letters to White are annotated: 'U-S for perusal,

HW' or: 'Dear Bayne – You may like to see this, HW'. They are always returned with a laconic: 'Tks, CGB', the first known examples of my grandfather's handwriting. Donald Smeaton's appointment, however, was less successful. His book *The Loyal Karens of Burma*, published in 1887, was highly critical of British policy. Smeaton wrote: 'The annexation of the upper country will not be the unmixed blessing either to ourselves or to the people which many seem to suppose.' Even in Lower Burma, he argued: 'The Burmese people bitterly resent the overthrow of their monarchy. They look upon this as the destruction of their nationality. Whether we have acted wisely history will decide.' The outspoken Smeaton constantly clashed with his chief in the months ahead.

Crosthwaite wanted to put the new province's finances on a firm footing as soon as possible. He successfully bid for the appointment of a Financial Commissioner, another new post. Crosthwaite originally intended this for Donald Smeaton, but apparently changed his mind and it went instead to Frederic Fryer, whom Bernard had brought in from the Punjab in 1886 to be a Commissioner in Upper Burma. Fryer already had a financial background and on his arrival in June 1888 Crosthwaite put him to work at once on drafting a Land Revenue Regulation for Upper Burma. The position of Director for Land Records and Agriculture was revived and given to William Hall. But Sir Charles Crosthwaite also relied at times on Charles Bayne as his economic expert. When he went to Calcutta in December 1888 to pay a farewell call on Lord Dufferin, he hoped to agree a budget settlement for Burma with the Financial Member of the Viceroy's Council. He took Charles Bayne with him rather than Fryer or Hall, though in the event he wrote to White on 5 December: 'I am sending Bayne back as the Financial Member does not desire to fleece us at present. He is disinclined to make a contract – he thinks our affairs too uncertain. Lord Dufferin as usual very affable, I believe he is well satisfied.' Charles Bayne had to travel back to Rangoon with Edward Moylan, the hostile correspondent of *The Times*, on whom more below.

To Crosthwaite's relief, Smeaton went off on furlough in August 1888. Herbert White became officiating Chief Secretary, with Charles Bayne as Secretary, and their workload was heavy. White records:

> 'These were years of abnormal stress in the office, which was still under-manned. The appointment of Mr Fryer to be Financial Commissioner afforded some relief. But part of the revenue business necessarily was transacted by the Secretariat. These were my really strenuous years. Day after day, Sundays included, I did my spell of work in office and then wrote far into the night at home, kept awake by coffee and protected from mosquitoes by Burman cheroots. Six hours of sleep sufficed.'

Charles Bayne, promoted to Deputy Commissioner in November, no doubt worked just as hard. The notes between them continued: 'Sec'y for perusal and return, HW; Tks, CGB.' Sir Charles Crosthwaite was clearly very satisfied with their performance. Donald Smeaton returned from leave and so did Edward Symes – still unmarried, despite Sir Charles Bernard urging him to find a wife. But Crosthwaite kept White and Bayne at their Secretariat posts and used Symes and Smeaton as Commissioners in Upper Burma. The Burma government as in early 1890 is shown in Table 4.1.

Restoring Civil Administration

Sir Charles Crosthwaite's great achievement was the pacification of Burma and the establishment of settled civil administration throughout the province. This task would occupy all of his four years in Burma. When he arrived, an uneasy quiet prevailed in Lower Burma. But there was persistent unrest in Upper Burma, where British rule at best covered the central lowland region and did not extend to the frontiers. There was no centrally organised resistance movement, but separate

Table 4.1.   The Government of British Burma, January 1890

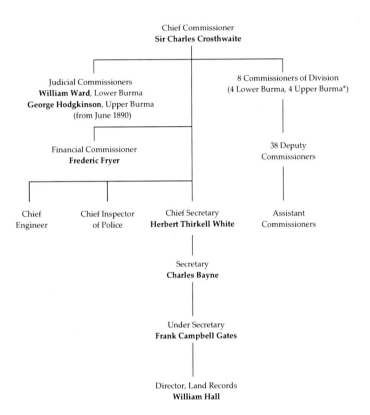

Chief Commissioner
Sir Charles Crosthwaite

Judicial Commissioners
William Ward, Lower Burma
George Hodgkinson, Upper Burma
(from June 1890)

8 Commissioners of Division
(4 Lower Burma, 4 Upper Burma*)

Financial Commissioner
Frederic Fryer

38 Deputy
Commissioners

Chief
Engineer

Chief Inspector
of Police

Chief Secretary
Herbert Thirkell White

Assistant
Commissioners

Secretary
Charles Bayne

Under Secretary
Frank Campbell Gates

Director, Land Records
William Hall

* Divisions of Lower Burma: Arakan, Irrawaddy, Pegu, Tenasserim
Divisions of Upper Burma: Northern, Eastern, Southern, Central

28

bands of rebels controlled large areas and easily eluded the colonial troops sent after them. Once the troops had moved on, the rebels would return and exact retribution on any Burmese who had collaborated with the colonial power.

Crosthwaite addressed these problems in his usual forceful and systematic fashion. To secure the whole territory of Burma he first sent expeditions into the Shan hills to obtain the submission of the local princes. Most of them were confirmed in office but warned to keep the peace among themselves. Later columns penetrated the country occupied by Chins and Kachins and established a presence on the Chinese frontier. A second strand of Crosthwaite's policy was to establish an efficient police force throughout the province. He had already formed a low opinion of the police in Lower Burma as being 'the worst and the most costly in the world'. He now got Lord Dufferin's authority for the formation of regiments of military police, recruited in India, who would maintain law and order in both parts of the province. Their numbers built up rapidly, to reach their full complement of 18,000 officers and men during 1888, and then remained stable at that level. As military police posts were established in both Upper and Lower Burma, regular army units could be withdrawn.

Rebellion and brigandage persisted in many areas, however, with outbreaks quite close to Rangoon and Mandalay. Crosthwaite decided that one reason was the easy availability of firearms and ordered the disarming of the entire province, starting in September 1887. A second reason was that villages, either through fear or tacit sympathy, would secretly shelter bands of insurgents and their leaders or conceal information about their movements. In these cases Crosthwaite, from May 1888 onwards, would order offending villages to be uprooted and resettled in places where they could be kept under surveillance.

Crosthwaite accepted the drawbacks of this policy but decided he had no alternative. 'The grouping of villages has unfortunately no legal sanction,' he wrote to White in August 1888, 'but it is necessary to do it if the dacoit groups are to be broken up'. A year later he concluded: 'There has been some injudicious moving of villages, but not much, and there has been some neglect of the deported people. I can't help it. But we should never have succeeded without these methods'. By such measures the insurgency was brought under control, with the leaders killed or imprisoned and the bands dispersed.

To reinforce the stability of both parts of the province, Crosthwaite introduced an entirely new system of local administration. In his view, the failure of the Lower Burma police was linked to the reliance on the *thugyi* system left over from the monarchy. In Upper Burma law and order had already broken down under Thibaw, while many of the *thugyis* had been involved in the insurgency. Even before taking up his post, Crosthwaite had gained Lord Dufferin's backing for the appointment of a headman in every village, to be responsible for law and order and tax collection. This was the system with which he was familiar from thirty years' experience in India. He had headmen installed throughout the villages of Upper Burma as the pacification proceeded, with a parallel conversion in Lower Burma. The reform reunited legal and tax collecting powers, though at a lower level than the traditional *thugyi*. Moreover, the headman owed his authority to the colonial power, not to the respect of his community. The system was embodied in the Upper Burma Village Regulation of 1887 and the Burma Village Act of 1889 and was steadily introduced throughout the province.

Responding to Criticism

There were thus heavy demands on the Secretariat, who had to prepare the measures needed to bring Upper Burma under British rule and to reform the entire system of provincial administration at local level. They also had to respond to widespread public attacks on Crosthwaite's policies, especially the uprooting of villages. The local newspapers, the *Rangoon Times* and *Rangoon Gazette*, were always ready to find fault with the colonial government. More seriously, the Rangoon correspondent of *The Times*, Edward Moylan, was a persistent hostile critic, reflecting the views of the minority in Britain that disapproved of the annexation and believed the colonial power only too capable of injustice and brutality. Crosthwaite worried about Moylan's attacks throughout his time in Burma. As soon as White and Bayne took over as Chief Secretary and Secretary in August 1888, he ordered them: 'I must have my answer ready against the falsehoods spread by the local journals and by Moylan.' Two weeks later he was writing: "Please do get all the refutations of Moylan put together as quickly as possible in pamphlet form'. Herbert White annotates the letter: 'Dear Bayne – Can we push these refutations through? The pamphlet seems to have taken CC's fancy', while he reassures Crosthwaite: 'Sec'y's attending to this'. So Charles Bayne became responsible for a pioneering example of what is familiar today as 'public diplomacy'.

The attacks, however, came not only from the press, but also from Crosthwaite's own senior staff. Donald Smeaton was the most articulate. He had already condemned the idea of Crosthwaite's local reforms in *The Loyal Karens*, saying: 'We have failed to seize the spirit of self-government in the East. We would supplant all indigenous processes by patents of our own'. Crosthwaite had to rebuke him sternly in 1889 and wrote to White in August 1890: 'Smeaton has taken umbrage with me and rudely repelled any offer of kindness. He is crazy, I think.' But Smeaton could be discounted as an outsider. Much more serious opposition came from the original members of the Burma Commission, who attacked both Crosthwaite's harsh measures against the insurgency and his reforms of local administration.

George Hodgkinson emerged as the leading figure in this movement after he returned to Rangoon in May 1888 as Commissioner for the Pegu division. Crosthwaite wrote in exasperation to White in August:

'You know the difficulties I am under. Look at the view so readily taken by Smeaton and Hodgkinson. I am disheartened sometimes by the feeling, in fact knowledge, that many of the men in the Commission are opposed to disarming or any strong measures. Some of them – not Hodgkinson, who is perfectly straight – are I believe positively disloyal and help the enemy.'

This tension between Crosthwaite and Hodgkinson created a difficult dilemma for Charles Bayne. He was a member of Sir Charles Crosthwaite's personal staff and owed him complete loyalty. Crosthwaite trusted him to prepare the public defence of his policies. But George Hodgkinson was his earliest patron, to whom he owed his advancement in his career. More than that, Charles Bayne was by now courting his youngest sister Augusta. It cannot have been easy for him to hear his future brother-in-law attacked in the office during the day and his chief criticised when he visited his fiancée in the evening. No doubt he kept his head down and his mouth shut, as far as he could.

However, thanks to his diplomatic skill and equable temperament he was clearly able to retain the confidence and friendship of both parties. He worked faithfully for Sir Charles Crosthwaite for another eighteen months, while gaining George Hodgkinson's consent to marry his Augusta. Crosthwaite then agreed he could go on furlough at once after the wedding in January 1890, with Frank Gates taking his place as Secretary. Herbert White also got three months leave later in the year, as Crosthwaite wrote to him: 'If Bayne will take leave as soon as he can, Gates could get into the work before you go.' When a libel case was being prepared against Edward Moylan, Crosthwaite told White: 'I send this to you as Bayne will probably be occupied with his own affairs.'

Sir Charles Crosthwaite himself needed leave in 1889, when Anthony MacDonnell officiated for him. But he returned 'full of work as usual', according to Frederic Fryer's diary. By the end of 1890 his work of pacification was complete and calm prevailed throughout the province. In December he handed over to Sir Alexander Mackenzie as Chief Commissioner and left Burma. He went on to become Lieutenant Governor of the North-West Provinces and Oudh and a member of the Council for India in London. Herbert White later wrote in praise of him:

'He was above all a great and strong administrator. Without the untiring industry and attention to minute detail of Sir Charles Bernard, the subtle brain of Lord MacDonnell, the almost inconceivable rapidity of Sir Alexander Mackenzie, to mention some of his contemporaries, he excelled them all as a ruler and leader of men. Fearless, robust, resolute, clear-sighted, he was admirably fitted for the great work which he accomplished in Burma. His judgement of men was good; his officers might rely on him for the fullest support in difficulties. He was a chief under whom it was a pleasure to serve, a friend who never failed.'

Charles Bayne too would have admired his chief and he kept in touch with him over the years ahead. But he would have recognised the force of the criticisms made by Moylan, Smeaton and his brother-in-law George Hodgkinson.

Table 5. 1   **Family Tree of the Hodgkinsons**

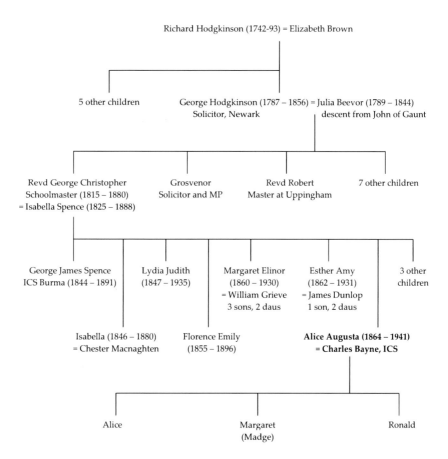

Richard Hodgkinson (1742-93) = Elizabeth Brown

5 other children

George Hodgkinson (1787 – 1856) = Julia Beevor (1789 – 1844)
Solicitor, Newark   descent from John of Gaunt

Revd George Christopher
Schoolmaster (1815 – 1880)
= Isabella Spence (1825 – 1888)

Grosvenor
Solicitor and MP

Revd Robert
Master at Uppingham

7 other children

George James Spence
ICS Burma (1844 – 1891)

Lydia Judith
(1847 – 1935)

Margaret Elinor
(1860 – 1930)
= William Grieve
3 sons, 2 daus

Esther Amy
(1862 – 1931)
= James Dunlop
1 son, 2 daus

3 other
children

Isabella (1846 – 1880)
= Chester Macnaghten

Florence Emily
(1855 – 1896)

Alice Augusta (1864 – 1941)
= Charles Bayne, ICS

Alice

Margaret
(Madge)

Ronald

Chapter 5

Personal Interlude:
Courtship, Marriage and Family

It is now time to look more closely at the family of my grandmother, Alice Augusta Hodgkinson – see family tree in Table 5.1. The Hodgkinsons had become established in Lincolnshire and Nottinghamshire by the 17th century. The first George Hodgkinson (1787-1856), fifth son of Richard Hodgkinson of Morton Grange, became a solicitor in Newark and married Julia Beevor, who could trace her descent back to John of Gaunt. Their second son, Grosvenor (1818-1871) took on the solicitor's practice and became MP for Newark. Their eldest, George Christopher Hodgkinson (1815-1880 – my great-grandfather) chose to take Anglican orders and enter the teaching profession. He took his degree from Trinity College, Cambridge, where he narrowly failed to get a Fellowship and became famous for an athletic exploit. Having bet that he could shoot 12 pigeons, jump five hurdles, leap another five on horseback, scull a mile and run a mile all in less than 30 minutes, he completed the course easily with eight minutes in hand. He became an active mountaineer and was an early member of the Alpine Club.

In his teaching career, from 1840 onwards, he was successively Principal of Hull College; second master at King Edward School, Bury St Edmunds; Principal of the Royal Agricultural College, Cirencester; and Principal of the Diocesan Training Institution at York. While at York in 1854, he was accused of introducing erroneous high church doctrines. An enquiry conducted by the Archbishop of York and Bishop of Ripon pronounced him blameless. Even so, he left to become headmaster of King Edward VI Grammar School in Louth, near the Lincolnshire coast, and stayed there for the next 25 years. On retirement in 1879 he became Rector of Screveton near Nottingham and lived in the adjacent village of Car Colston, where he died a year later.

George Christopher Hodgkinson married Isabella Lydia Spence, niece of James Clark Ross and great-niece of John Ross, the polar explorers. The couple had ten surviving children, three boys and seven girls. The eldest son, George James Spence Hodgkinson, born in 1845, successfully took the exam for the ICS in 1868, after being coached by his father, who published a pamphlet proposing changes in the system. George James went out to Bengal and served at Sarun and Tirhut, in hill country beyond the Ganges, north of Calcutta. He invited his eldest sister Isabella (born 1846) to join him and she stayed on while he became the manager of the local maharajah's estates at Hutwah. On 11 June 1872 Bella was married at Tirhut to Chester Macnaghten of the Bombay Education Service. The couple went off to Gujerat, where Chester Macnaghten was Principal of Rajkumar College at Rajkot. He stayed there till he retired 24 years later, but sadly Bella died in 1880; they had no children.

Two more Hodgkinson daughters, Lydia Judith (born 1847) and Florence Emily (born 1855) stayed at home as spinsters, while Edith Selena (born 1854) married and went to New Zealand. But after George James moved to Burma in 1878, as officiating Commissioner for Arakan, the fifth Hodgkinson girl, Margaret Elinor (born 1860), came out to join him. The expatriate circle at Akyab, the divisional capital of Arakan, included J. B. Grieve, the local partner for Bulloch Brothers, rice merchants, shippers and insurance agents. His brother William Grieve, a Rangoon partner in the firm, met and courted Margaret and married her at Akyab on 11 September 1880.

This was a happier event for George James and Margaret, in a year that had earlier seen the deaths of their father in April far away at Car Colston and their sister Bella in June at Rajkote on the other side of India. The Grieves set up house in Rangoon and their first two children were born there in 1881 and 1883. In the following year they moved back to England, as William Grieve became a London partner in the firm.

Isabella Lydia Hodgkinson, George Christopher's widow, lived on till February 1888 and probably her two youngest daughters, Esther Amy (born 1862) and Alice Augusta – Gussie – (born 1864) stayed with her. But after her death they too were free to join the 'fishing fleet'. They came out to stay with their brother George James once he had moved back to Rangoon in May 1888 as Commissioner for Pegu. He had a wide circle of friends and his match-making skills were undiminished. The first evidence of Charles Bayne's wooing of Augusta appears in August, when Sir Charles Crosthwaite ended a letter to Herbert White: 'Give my love to Bayne. I have naught special to say to him. He will be getting married next.'

Thereafter the clues to events in the Hodgkinson family come from the diary of Frederic Fryer. As Financial Commissioner, Fryer worked in the same building as Herbert White and Charles Bayne, but they were ten to fifteen years junior to him. So he hardly ever mentions them and never invites them to dinner, though his wife sometimes went out with Mrs White – they were both called Frances (Fanny). He was, however, an exact contemporary of George Hodgkinson, both in age and entry to the Bengal service. They were soon in regular contact, not only for official business but also for social occasions. Frederic Fryer first mentions the Hodgkinson sisters in February 1889, when he invites them to dinner after a business session with George. Tennis at the Hodgkinsons in May and dinner there in August follow in Fryer's diary. Then, on 27 September, the Fryers give a dinner for Anthony MacDonnell, the officiating Chief Commissioner, and the other guests include 'Bayne and two Miss Hodgkinsons'. This diary entry shows that, despite the heavy pressures of work in the Secretariat and the coolness between Crosthwaite and George Hodgkinson, Charles Bayne has successfully pursued his romance with Augusta. He has proposed and she has accepted him. The Fryers have therefore invited him – for the first time – as Augusta's official fiancé, with Esther Amy there as her chaperone in George's absence.

George Hodgkinson no doubt hoped and expected that Esther Amy, as the elder sister, would be the first to marry. Like Margaret Elinor ten years before, she was courted by a Rangoon member of Bulloch Brothers, James Bourne Dunlop. James and Esther Amy were married in Christchurch, Rangoon, on 30 October 1889. The Fryers were at the wedding and afterwards at the reception at George Hodgkinson's house, where they presented two lamps they had bought the day before. Augusta would have been part of the family party and Charles Bayne was no doubt there too. The Dunlops left Rangoon at once for Murree in the Punjab, where James had a new job as manager of the Alliance Bank of Simla. Their two daughters were born there in 1891 and 1893.

Three months later Augusta was married to Charles Bayne on 29 January 1890 in Christchurch, Rangoon. A photo survives of my grandmother in her wedding dress and veil, sewn with flowers (Plate II). Frederic Fryer could not be there this time, as he was supporting Sir Charles Crosthwaite in Mandalay. It seems that George Hodgkinson was also absent, since he did not sign the register as he had at Esther's wedding. He too may have been summoned to Mandalay by Crosthwaite; otherwise a sudden illness or a crisis in Pegu division must have kept him away. Colonel Horace Spearman, the present Commissioner for Irrawaddy division, signed in his place. He was a long-standing colleague of George Hodgkinson's and had been Charles Bayne's first Deputy Commissioner at Henzada, nine years before. Two other witnesses must have been chosen as Charles Bayne's friends. Daniel Twomey was a Secretariat colleague, who would soon move up to become Under Secretary. William Bigge, first judge in the Small Cause Court, was a protégé of Frederic Fryer.

Immediately after the wedding Charles Bayne took his bride back home on furlough. Charles would have found many changes in his family. His father Peter Bayne had moved from Kilburn to Norwood and married again. We do not know the name of his third wife; it may be that Charles and his brother Ronald, now vicar of Orlestone in Kent, disapproved of her. His sister Clotilda was engaged to the Rev Charles Marson, who had gone to Australia for his health. Charles would just have had time to see her before she left for Adelaide, where she was married in June. The couple also spent time in Nottinghamshire with Augusta's sisters Lydia and Florence. There her marriage settlement was drawn up, with the help of the family solicitors, Hodgkinson and Beevor of Newark, founded by Augusta's grandfather. Augusta's signature on the deed was witnessed by her eldest sister Lydia and Charles' by Grosvenor Hodgkinson, Augusta's solicitor cousin. The Rev Ronald Bayne and George James Hodgkinson were the other trustees and the deed took effect from 26 March 1891.

George Hodgkinson signed the deed at his new base in Mandalay. He had moved there in March 1890, first on special duty to review the sentences of captive rebels and later as Judicial Commissioner for Upper Burma, a newly established post. But the friction persisted between him and Sir Charles Crosthwaite, who had opposed the creation of a Judicial Commissioner while Upper Burma was still unsettled. He regarded Hodgkinson as much too lenient, writing to Herbert White on 20 August 1890: 'Hodgkinson gave me a scare. I am afraid he will lose his head as JC. The glory of letting fellows off seems too much for most men.'

The Baynes had hoped to spend nearly two years in England. But after Sir Alexander Mackenzie replaced Crosthwaite as Chief Commissioner, Charles Bayne was called back to Rangoon to take up the post of Secretary again from 10 March

1891, on a confirmed basis. By early that year Augusta was heavily pregnant and she evidently sent off Charles on his own. She remained in England for the birth of their first daughter, Alice Lydia, on 2 February 1891. The birth was registered in Kensington, which suggests that Augusta was staying with her sister Margaret Elinor Grieve. It is not clear when Augusta and the baby were reunited with Charles in Rangoon. European women were scarce in Burma, because the climate was reckoned to be especially unhealthy for them, as the next chapter will show. Fanny Thirkell White was unusual in staying with her husband throughout his career of 32 years.

Burma could be unhealthy for European men too. On 28 December 1891 George Hodgkinson died suddenly in Mandalay, from a stroke (the burial register says 'apoplexy'). The railway link between Rangoon and Mandalay had been completed two years before and Charles would at once have taken the train north to attend the impressive official funeral on the following day. Charles Bayne was the chief mourner, supported by George Burgess, the Commissioner for the Mandalay division, who would take over as the next Judicial Commissioner for Upper Burma. It is not clear if Augusta came too and she might still have been in England. She is not mentioned in the report of the funeral and the wreath on the coffin was from Mrs Burgess. But if Augusta was there, she would have joined Charles among the 'large number of gentlemen and sprinkling of ladies assembled at "Salween House", the residence of the late Mr Hodgkinson' after the ceremony.

George Hodgkinson's obituary provides a conventional statement of his public and private virtues. He was a just man and a sound lawyer, who seasoned justice with mercy. He brought system to judicial work in Upper Burma, correcting scandals and abuses. He was unostentatious, even retiring, in manner and charitable in his actions. His personal life was 'a pattern which the officials of a country which has acquired such a notorious reputation as Burma would do well to follow'. The obituary concludes: 'In his sudden death the government have suffered the loss of a tried and brilliant servant'. But it hardly does justice to his achievements and his potential. George Hodgkinson had served as Commissioner in all four divisions of Lower Burma, as well as Judicial Commissioner with responsibility for the whole of Upper Burma. Sir Charles Bernard in effect made him Chief Commissioner for Lower Burma in 1886-7, when he was preoccupied with the war in the north. Like Bernard, George Hodgkinson favoured a conciliatory approach to colonial administration, making the most of local talent and respecting local customs. Inevitably, he clashed with the autocratic style of Sir Charles Crosthwaite, who preferred to impose solutions from outside. But even Crosthwaite respected his integrity.

When George Hodgkinson died, aged 46, he had already served 23 years with the ICS and could soon have retired on his pension. But had he lived, he would have been eligible to succeed Sir Alexander Mackenzie as the next Chief Commissioner. He would probably have filled the post with greater distinction than his contemporary Frederic Fryer, who was in fact chosen. So I honour the memory of my great-uncle George, just as Charles and Augusta must have mourned a good friend and colleague and a faithful brother, to whom they owed so much.

Chapter 6

Revenue Secretary in the 1890s

Sir Alexander Mackenzie as Chief Commissioner
As soon as he took over as Chief Commissioner in December 1890, Sir Alexander Mackenzie reorganised his central administration, setting a pattern that would endure for the rest of the decade. Edward Symes and Donald Smeaton came back to Rangoon: the first was Chief Secretary till his death in 1901; the second succeeded Frederic Fryer as Financial Commissioner and stayed till he retired in 1902. Charles Bayne and Frank Gates are shown in the official lists as Secretary and Junior Secretary, until Bayne becomes Revenue Secretary in March 1893, with Gates moving up to be Secretary.

In fact, Charles Bayne must have held the local rank of Revenue Secretary right from his return from leave. The *Report on the Administration of Burma* for 1890-1 records 'the appointment of an additional Secretary in December 1890', while Sir Alexander Mackenzie mentions the Revenue Secretary in a note of May 1892. The Resolutions transmitting to Calcutta the Reports on Revenue Administration, Forests and Excise were signed by Herbert White as officiating Chief Secretary up to 1890. But they were signed in 1891 and 1892 by Charles Bayne as Secretary and thereafter by him as Revenue Secretary. Apart from a break for two years furlough, he remained Revenue Secretary, with Frank Gates as Secretary, till early 1899. Thus throughout the decade he was responsible for a wide range of economic policies, which grew in importance now that the province was calm. The content of these policies will be considered in the next chapter.

On 21 March 1892 Edward Symes went off on three months privilege leave and Charles Bayne became officiating Chief Secretary. It was the first time he had taken charge of the whole Secretariat and it proved a tragic and taxing time. Sir Alexander Mackenzie had come to Rangoon with his wife Georgina, to whom he had been married for nearly 30 years. At this time she fell fatally ill and died sometime in April. Sir Alexander wound up his affairs in the province in great haste and left for 18 months home leave on 4 May, possibly taking his wife's body with him – there is no record of her burial in Burma. Before he left, however, he had time to prepare and sign off a ten-page 'Note for my Locum Tenens', with supporting papers on the opium trade and other issues; much of this material must have been prepared by Charles Bayne. Mackenzie adds a note to his opium memo, which is dated 30 April: 'I have had to draw up this minute under great pressure of time and at a time of grave domestic trouble and on the eve of my departure from the province'.

Donald Smeaton took over at once as officiating Chief Commissioner, but was clearly not considered more than a stop-gap. The post was offered first to Anthony MacDonnell, who declined it, and then to Frederic Fryer, who had gone back to the Punjab after a year's leave. Fryer accepted and was called at once to Simla for briefing from the Viceroy, Lord Lansdowne, and others. He then went on to take a 'beastly boat' from Calcutta for a rough crossing – 'I could not eat my dinner' – arriving on 22 May to find 'all Rangoon on the wharf to meet us'.

Charles Bayne was still officiating Chief Secretary and would have prepared detailed briefing for Fryer's arrival. But he gets little recognition for it from Fryer's diary, beyond a note on 3 June: 'Bayne came this morning'. On 27 June Edward Symes returned from leave and Charles Bayne no doubt went back with great relief to being Revenue Secretary. For the rest of

1892 he only appears once in Fryer's diary, when on 3 November 'Bayne and Gates came as usual'. There is no suggestion, now or later, that Fryer disliked him. But he never got into Fryer's inner circle for a simple reason; he did not ride, or at least not for pleasure. Frederic Fryer was tremendously keen on horses, kept a large stable and his diary is full of rides, drives and other equine matters. Edward Symes was likewise an active rider; he played polo and had a horse called Ambition whom Fryer sometimes borrowed. Frank Gates, who accompanied the Chief Commissioner on long travels through Burma in the summer of 1892 and again to Moulmein in December, was also a horseman. As a result, Symes and Gates (both unmarried) often went out riding with the Fryers. They became regular dinner guests at Government House, while there is no sign from the diary that the Baynes ever did.

Frederic Fryer was keen on all forms of sport. In 1892 he only notes one session of lawn tennis (with Edward Symes), but in 1893 it becomes a favoured diversion, either at Government House or at the Smeatons'. Fortunately Charles Bayne was a competent tennis player. He appears three times in tennis parties at Government House in March 1893, with Augusta also present on one occasion, and is named again as a tennis partner later in the year. But he still does not accompany Frederic Fryer on his travels, according to Fryer's diary, or get invited to dinner. The great event for Burma in 1893 was the visit of the Viceroy in November, right at the end of his term of office. When Lord Lansdowne and his wife arrived in Rangoon on 17 November by ship, Fryer 'went on board and dined and slept. Smeaton and Symes went with me.' The Viceroy's party went on to Mandalay and to Bhamo in the far north, with Frederic Fryer in attendance, but no sign of Charles Bayne. His main concern would have been the birth of his second daughter, Margaret Clotilda (Madge) on 22 November. She was born in Rangoon (her birth was not registered in England) but not baptised there; the Baynes must have delayed this till their next home leave.

Sir Alexander Mackenzie had his leave extended to two years and found a new wife, Mabel Elliott. He had hoped not to be sent back to Burma again, but instead to move into a place on the Viceroy's Council that became vacant in 1893. Lord Lansdowne wrote to him on 4 July: 'I take note of your statement that it would be distasteful to you to return to Burma and that you would be glad if some other arrangement could be made to provide you with a suitable appointment'. But this plan was upset by a disagreement over opium policy. Mackenzie's minute of 30 April 1892 had endorsed recommendations from Donald Smeaton for introducing a new opium regime in Burma. Hitherto opium had been available to non-Burmans, especially Chinese, but illegal for Burmans. The puritan Smeaton wanted all sales of opium banned, except for medicinal purposes, and Mackenzie supported him, though it was against Indian government policy. This led to a sharp exchange of letters with Lord Lansdowne, who ended by giving the vacant place on his Council to Anthony MacDonnell. So Sir Alexander Mackenzie had to return to Rangoon with his second wife Mabel in May 1894. Frederic Fryer went back to the Punjab to officiate as Financial Commissioner there. But Mackenzie ensured that the good work Fryer and Donald Smeaton had done in his absence was recognised. Fryer became a Knight Commander of the Star of India (KCSI) and Smeaton a Companion of the Order (CSI) in January 1895.

In his first letter from Rangoon to the new Viceroy, Lord Elgin, on 5 May, Sir Alexander Mackenzie comments on the sickness prevalent among his staff. 'I am sorry to find so many officers sick and asking for leave. My Chief Secretary, Mr Symes, is I think seriously out of health and the Civil Surgeon cannot account for his symptoms. I fear they indicate brain trouble from over-work. The other two Secretaries are chronic invalids' – meaning Charles Bayne and Frank Gates. A month later Mackenzie writes: 'The heat here is very trying. Every week some officer breaks down. My Chief Secretary, Mr Symes, will hardly be able to hold out till July. If he should go to Simla on his way home, I think your Excellency would find it interesting to talk to him. He is a man of great local experience and wonderfully good judgement.' Edward Symes in fact got away safely in July to start two years furlough. Charles Bayne and Frank Gates evidently recovered – we hear no more of their being ill. But Edward Symes' condition would prove more serious.

Mackenzie called back Herbert White, who was now the divisional Commissioner at Mandalay, to officiate as Chief Secretary in Symes' absence. It is a bit odd that Charles Bayne was not asked to do this, as he had done two years before. It may simply be that he too was due for furlough in six months time and Mackenzie wanted more continuity. But it could also mean that Charles Bayne was too closely associated in Mackenzie's mind with the tragedy of his first wife's death. Herbert White gives a vivid picture of the Secretariat at work at this time:

'The Province was in order and the Secretariat was administered on more regular lines than in the earlier strenuous years. It was no longer necessary to burn the midnight oil or to abjure exercise and recreation. Sir Alexander Mackenzie was a man of extraordinary capacity and of abnormal, in my experience unexampled, speed of work. Throughout the day four Secretaries toiled and filled office boxes with files; by nine o'clock next morning all came back with his orders noted on them. He left the Secretaries to do their own work and wrote less than any other chief I have known. But he was the strong man, the mainspring and motive-power of the administration.'

Herbert White continues with a general comment on the power of the Secretariat and its limits, which also deserves quoting:

'No Secretary cherished the delusion that he was running the Province. In Burma the theory that Secretaries are supreme has no foundation in fact. The power and subtle intrigues ascribed to provincial secretariats are the vain imaginings of people who have had no experience of their working from within. I must confess that life in the Secretariat, interesting enough to the workers, presented few incidents likely to enthral the most sympathetic reader. The more smoothly the machinery worked, the fewer sparks were thrown off.'

Charles Bayne, I believe, would have agreed with every word.

Once again, however, the health of his family distracted Sir Alexander Mackenzie and led to an early departure. His wife safely gave birth to a healthy boy in August 1894, for whom Lady Elgin, the new Vicereine, stood godmother. But in mid-August Mabel Mackenzie 'had rather a bad turn', as Sir Alexander writes to Lord Elgin: 'I am a good deal worried about her. My little son flourishes exceedingly.' She remained very weak for the next three months, giving her husband 'a weary and harassing time', and did not properly recover till she moved away to the drier climate of Meiktila, Upper Burma, in November. Sir Alexander did not want to take any more risks with his wife's health. On 21 February 1895 he reported to the Viceroy that doctors in London, consulted by her mother, advised that she should leave Burma during the hot weather and rains. But Sir Alexander feared that if he had to ask for leave again so as to be with her, he might neither be allowed to return to Rangoon nor be offered another post; could the Viceroy reassure him?

Before Lord Elgin could reply, Mackenzie wrote again on 2 March: 'Our little boy was seized with dysentery while I was away inspecting Bassein. I got back here to find his mother broken down with anxiety and the doctor said he was too susceptible to the Burma climate and would have to be moved away.' Mackenzie arranged a passage out for them on 13 April, but told Elgin: 'I fear it will be very difficult to get the wife off by herself. The idea of a sea voyage brings on hysteria and fainting; and I am most sorely tried.' Lord Elgin, however, proved more sympathetic to Mackenzie's concerns than his predecessor had been. Mackenzie was offered to become Home Member on the Viceroy's Council, which he gratefully accepted. The Mackenzie family left Rangoon on 3 April 1895 for the healthier climate of Simla. Sir Frederic Fryer, nothing loath, returned as Chief Commissioner again, this time on a confirmed basis. He would stay in Burma for another eight years, till April 1903.

Two Years Leave for the Baynes

But by the time all this was resolved, Charles and Augusta Bayne and the two girls had left for a second and longer spell of furlough, to which he was now entitled every three-four years. They sailed from Rangoon on 26 February 1895 and stayed away till December 1896. It was a sad time for Charles to be in England, as his father's third wife was declared insane and committed to an asylum late in 1895. This deeply affected the ailing Peter Bayne, who died in February 1896, aged 65. He was buried in Harlington churchyard, next to his first wife Clotilda, Charles's mother. Their joint tomb and the separate monument to Anna Bayne, his second wife and Charles's step-mother, survive there to this day, in an oasis of calm between Heathrow airport and the M4 motorway.

Charles and his elder brother Ronald would have been responsible for disposing of Peter Bayne's house in Norwood and sorting through all his books and papers, as he had contin-ued writing to the end. It may well have been this experience that stimulated Charles Bayne to develop the practice of histor-ical research that occupied him in retirement. Ronald would have encouraged him, since he combined his Anglican ministry with being a contributor to the *Dictionary of National Biography*, now being issued, while his edition of the Elizabethan play *Arden of Feversham* would be published in 1897.

Augusta Bayne also suffered a bereavement, as her sister Florence died in April 1896, aged only 41; she left many Burmese items in her will, evidently gifts from her widely trav-elled siblings. Now only Lydia Hodgkinson was left at the family home in Nottinghamshire, though two other married sisters – Margaret Grieve and Esther Dunlop – were back in England again. Later in 1896 Charles and Augusta had their photographs taken in a studio in Reigate and the pictures show the couple clearly refreshed by their leave. Charles appears alert, intelligent and humorous, while Augusta looks elegant and determined (Plates III and IV). As they left England in November 1896, Charles put his initials into a copy of Rudyard Kipling's *The Seven Seas*, published that year. He may have bought it himself, or Augusta may have given it to him as an early present for his 36th birthday. But the Baynes had to leave their elder daughter Alice behind in England with her aunt Lydia at Car Colston, as was normal for children from six or seven onwards in ICS families. She was photographed in Nottingham in September 1897.

Sir Frederic Fryer as Lieutenant Governor

Charles Bayne returned to find Sir Frederic Fryer installed as Chief Commissioner again, while Edward Symes, the Chief Secretary, was back from his leave. Two important changes had got under way during his absence. First, Lord Lansdowne's visit in 1893 had, after a long delay, prompted a change in Burma's status. From May 1897 the Chief Commissioner was elevated to Lieutenant Governor and the province was given some legislative capacity, vested in a Legislative Council, with five official and four non-official members. The Council members were appointed from August 1897, on two-year terms, and included the three Secretaries – Edward Symes, Charles Bayne and Frank Gates. Donald Smeaton, the Financial Commissioner, joined in 1898 when he returned from furlough and Charles Bayne was reappointed in August 1899. The non-official members comprised both European and Burmese notables, including the Kinwun Mingyi, formerly chief minister of King Thibaw. From now on the Legislative Council would meet two or three times a year, in December to January. But it seldom had much business to transact and the meetings were soon over.

The second change was the practice of moving senior members of the provincial government in the hot weather to the hill-station of Maymyo, a garrison town 3000 feet up in the Shan hills, East of Mandalay. Initially this required a two day trek from the rail-head at Mandalay, but in 1900 a branch line reached Maymo and continued towards the Chinese border. (In fact it never got further than Lashio, the headquarters of the administration of the Northern Shan states.) Sir Frederic Fryer intended moving to Maymyo, with his wife, in April 1897, but an outbreak of cholera delayed their arrival till August; they returned to Rangoon in late October. Edward Symes, as Chief Secretary, accompanied them and boxes came up from Rangoon, by rail to Mandalay and then by pony. Herbert Thirkell White, still Commissioner at Mandalay, also appeared with his wife; later in the year he was appointed to lead the Boundary Commission delimiting the border with China. A holiday atmosphere prevailed, with much riding (the Whites were also keen equestrians) and visits to inspect each other's building works – Symes had selected a fine site on a hill. Herbert White wrote nostalgically of Maymyo as 'a place of great charm and quiet beauty, more like a corner of Surrey than of Burma'.

In 1898 the Fryers reached Maymyo in mid-March, with Edward Symes, and stayed there till late October, interrupted by a long tour through Burma and a visit to Rangoon in July-August. Donald Smeaton and Herbert White, with their wives, paid shorter visits. Fryer, always ready to try a new sport, became very keen on golf after a couple of lessons from Smeaton, but his enthusiasm did not last. Apart from Symes, however, the other Secretaries did not come up to Maymyo in 1897 and 1898 and remained filling boxes in Rangoon. Charles Bayne continued outside the Lieutenant Governor's inner circle. He called on Fryer when his chief was in Rangoon, for meetings affecting his work, and there were occasional sessions of tennis. But he did not accompany Fryer on any visits in these years, while Frank Gates was with him again in

Moulmein in December 1898. There is still no sign that the Baynes were invited to dinner at Government House, though no doubt they took part in large formal occasions such as Lord Elgin's visit in November 1898. This again took place as the Viceroy was leaving office and the programme was an exact repetition of Lord Lansdowne's visit five years before. But it included an important conference on Burma's forests, covered in the next chapter.

I would not conclude from this that Charles Bayne felt he was being cold-shouldered by Sir Frederic Fryer and resented it. He never appears to be a very gregarious character and probably preferred to spend his time quietly in Rangoon with his family than accompanying his chief on provincial visits or dining at Government House. He would certainly not have wanted to be stuck in Maymyo in the summer of 1897, as on 23 August Charles and Augusta celebrated the birth of their only son Ronald Christopher, my father. Unlike his sisters, Ronald was baptised in Rangoon, on 29 October: his name is in the appropriate register and a photo survives of him in his christening robes, held in his mother's arms. The family was now living in No 14 Halpin Road, in the civil and military quarter. The house survived till the early 1960s, but was then demolished to make way for the Chinese embassy, surrounded by a huge red wall.

For part of 1898 Charles Bayne had duties elsewhere, which would have prevented him from being in Maymyo. From March to July he had his only posting to Upper Burma, when he officiated as Commissioner for the Meiktila division, while the incumbent was on leave. Meiktila was the south-eastern division of Upper Burma, due north from Rangoon, and occupied the Sittang river valley, through which the railway to Mandalay ran. Charles Bayne was back from Meiktila, however, for Ronald's first birthday. The earliest photo of the two of them, taken around this time, shows Ronald sitting on his father's lap in a Burmese garden, aged about one. Charles is smiling proudly at his son, but wears glasses and looks more strained than he had two years before (Plate V.1).

Meanwhile, the holiday atmosphere of Maymyo was darkened by tragedy. Early in 1898 George Burgess, who had succeeded George Hodgkinson as Judicial Commissioner for Upper Burma, was taken ill. He took three months privilege leave and got back to Mandalay on 21 June. But within a week, as Fryer wrote in his diary, 'Burgess has had to go home at once on medical certificate'. He sailed from Rangoon on the SS *Derbyshire* and on Thursday 7 July Fryer recorded: 'Burgess was missed from the *Derbyshire* on Sunday last and is supposed to have fallen overboard'. Edward Symes and Herbert White knew Burgess well, as they had all served together in the Secretariat: Symes took over as Secretary from him. According to White, 'Mr Burgess's health was undermined by excessive work in the Secretariat'. Herbert White himself became the new Judicial Commissioner for Upper Burma, while George Scott (who will feature in Chapter 8) took over the Boundary Commission. But Burgess's death had a wider impact than some consequential career moves. Though Fryer would not believe it and White conceals it, George Burgess had in fact committed suicide.

Chapter 7

Managing Burma's Economy – Rice and Teak

After the turbulence of the pacification of Burma in the previous decade, the 1890s could be devoted to the peaceful development of the province and promoting its economic prosperity. This was Charles Bayne's professional responsibility. By far the most important economic activity in Burma was agriculture and specifically rice farming, which was concentrated in Lower Burma. Up to 80 per cent of the Burmese population gained their living from agriculture. Rice in turn made up 80 per cent of the province's exports. Taxes on agricultural land provided the principal source of revenue for the provincial government, as they had for the Kingdom of Burma. They were levied on the basis of the land settlement and registration system introduced by Donald Smeaton more than ten years earlier. Settlements were now being conducted in Upper Burma, as well as revised in Lower Burma.

Within the provincial government direct responsibility for land and revenue matters lay with the Financial Commissioner, the post held by Donald Smeaton throughout the 1890s. But Charles Bayne, as Revenue Secretary, prepared the issues put to the Chief Commissioner (later Lieutenant Governor) and drafted any recommendations he might make to the Indian government in Calcutta. As Sir Alexander Mackenzie said in his Note of 3 May 1892: 'Usually he [the Financial Secretary] has sent his own proposals to me through the Revenue Secretary and I have passed orders thereon'.

Rice Cultivation

The Burmese rural economy was booming in this period, thanks to strong demand for rice imports in both India and Europe. The acreage under cultivation for rice all over the Irrawaddy delta had been expanding steadily since the 1870s and the opening of the Suez Canal, while the population of Lower Burma had been increasing in parallel. This growth gathered pace in the period when Charles Bayne was Revenue Secretary. Between 1890 and 1900 the cultivated area grew by 2.3 million acres and the population by one million people. By 1900 exports of rice had reached 2.5 million tons, making Burma by far the largest rice-exporting region in the world. As a result, rice production and trade generated great wealth, especially for the millers, traders, shippers and those involved in financing the various stages of this activity.

But the problem was that very little of this wealth enriched the Burmese cultivators of the rice. Traditionally they were accustomed to subsistence farming, which produced a small surplus that could be bartered for other necessities or luxuries or used for charitable purposes. In developing new holdings and producing for sale into a money economy, most of the rice farmers had gone deeply into debt to Burmese and Indian money-lenders against the security of their land. They were obliged to sell their surplus rice to the British firms that controlled the export trade, who did their best to keep prices low. When harvests were good, as happened for most of the 1890s, the cultivators survived well and were encouraged to expand. But when bad years came, Burmese cultivators that could not meet their debts were forced to surrender their land and become tenants instead, usually on short leases with no security of tenure. A further run of misfortune could reduce them to working as landless labourers. The growing economic hardship of the rice farmers, alongside the visible wealth of other communities, led to widespread discontent and contributed to a steady revival of lawlessness.

The policy of the provincial government had always been to protect the cultivators on land that they owned. Donald Smeaton understood the need for action both to prevent the alienation of land and to give a better deal for tenant farmers. *The Report on the Revenue Administration of Burma* for 1890-1, his first year as Financial Commissioner, sets out the problem trenchantly:

> 'Tenant occupancy is steadily increasing and rents are rising. It is important, both in the interest of the State and of the people, that a large and unproductive landlord class should not arise in Burma; that the arable land of the country should be so disposable that all the agricultural population may be enabled to share on equal terms; and that the growth of a purely dependent class living on the leavings of others should be checked. The Financial Commissioner is now considering the question and has submitted to the Chief Commissioner a draft Bill dealing with it'.

Sir Alexander Mackenzie approved of this initiative, though he left Burma before he could address it properly. The Resolution transmitting the Report to Calcutta, endorsed by Mackenzie and signed by Charles Bayne, took the view:

> 'Cultivators are alienating their land to money-lenders. A gradual process of expropriation of the cultivating population is going on and it is a matter for serious consideration whether steps should not be taken to protect Burman landowners by limiting their powers of alienation. The question is one of great importance and the Financial Commissioner is now maturing proposals for dealing with it by legislation.'

Over the next year Donald Smeaton drafted and circulated two bills, which reflected his puritan approach to the issue. With land values rising and credit freely available, he wrote:

> 'The Burman agriculturist will borrow more freely and therefore lose his land more rapidly and completely than now. To protect the Burman from his own imprudence, we must pre-

vent the permanent transfer of land to any but agriculturists. To do so we must destroy, or at least seriously impair, the credit of the Burman cultivator with the non-agricultural trader and money-lender.'

Smeaton's Agricultural Relief Bill provided that no transfer of land by a Burman agriculturist was valid unless approved by a Deputy Commissioner. His Tenancy Bill would permit tenants to purchase their holdings at a sum equal to no more than three years rent.

But when Frederic Fryer took over from Mackenzie during 1892 he adopted a different view. There were signs of professional rivalry here, as Frederic Fryer had been Donald Smeaton's predecessor as Financial Commissioner. There was also personal tension between the two men, as there had been between Smeaton and Crosthwaite, because Smeaton was no respecter of persons. The Resolution covering the *Report on the Revenue Administration* for 1891-2, again signed by Charles Bayne, records the launching of Smeaton's two bills. It then adds a fatal sentence, surely inserted by Fryer himself: 'Mr Fryer considers that legislation for the protection of tenants and cultivators from landlords and money-lenders in Burma is not a matter of great urgency and it will not be recommended without further deliberation.' This, however, drew a sharp rebuke from the Government of India, who pointed out the difficulties that had been caused elsewhere in India by the neglect of these agrarian problems.

Over the next few years Fryer and Smeaton eventually reached agreement on new measures to submit to Calcutta. In January 1896 Fryer sent in proposals that would give cultivators a right of pre-emption on any sale of land, forbid sales to non-agriculturists (ie money-lenders) and limit the terms of mortgages and leases. In the same year he circulated a tenancy bill giving occupancy rights to tenants remaining on land for twelve years and providing for fixed rents. But Calcutta did not react to the land alienation proposals and the tenancy bill provoked opposition in Burma. While Bayne and Smeaton were away on leave in mid-decade, there were more voices being heard that denied that there was an urgent problem, so that decisions were always postponed.

The Resolution for 1895-6, signed by Charles Bayne just as he returned, recorded: 'On the whole the Chief Commissioner considers that agricultural tenants are in no immediate danger of oppression, but that judicious legislation may prevent the growth of abuses. A draft bill for the protection of tenants has been circulated for the opinions of Revenue Officers.' The Resolution for 1896-7 took the view: 'It cannot be said at present that the land is passing to any extent out of the hands of the agriculturist classes.' Finally the Resolution for 1897-8 concluded:

> 'These figures support the view expressed by the Director of Land Records that, as far as the contest between the trader and the agriculturist is concerned, the agricultural landlord has more than held his own during the year under report. It seems probable that the increase in tenancies was due in great measure to immigration from Upper Burma of agriculturists who will probably develop in course of time into landholders.'

There was no sense of urgency and nothing was done.

When Donald Smeaton returned from furlough in early 1898 he was evidently furious that Fryer was content to let matters run into the sand. Fryer's diary for 13 February notes: 'Smeaton very queer in behaviour'. Later he records long conferences with Smeaton and Thomas Wilson, the Director for Land Records, during that summer. These led to a proposal from Fryer to Lord Elgin that Smeaton should visit Calcutta to discuss revenue matters and be made an 'additional member' of the Viceroy's Council for this purpose. Additional members representing provincial interests were now being created alongside the Executive Council and when all met together they became the Legislative Council of India.

Elgin agreed to nominate Smeaton, saying on 24 September: 'Burma has a right, I think, to a representative on the Viceroy's

Council in its turn and its turn has fairly come'. Fryer welcomed this, as it got the abrasive Smeaton off his back. He told the Viceroy that 'I hope soon to send up my suggestion on the tenancy question', the first time he mentions it in a letter to Elgin. Donald Smeaton was also pleased, as he hoped it would enable him to promote his case to succeed Fryer as Lieutenant Governor. From now on Smeaton would spend six months of each year in Calcutta, while David Norton officiated for him as Financial Commissioner. He seemed to lose interest in the plight of the Burmese rice-farmers.

When the scale of rice production and export, the number of rice farmers and the area being cultivated for rice were all increasing year by year, it was hard to believe that the condition of the cultivators was steadily getting worse. But later events would show that Donald Smeaton's analysis was accurate and that corrective measures were necessary. Though there is no direct evidence from this period, I am sure that Charles Bayne would have supported him on the substance of the problem. He had seen Smeaton at work in this field since 1883 and he had worked in the rice-growing areas of Lower Burma himself, which Fryer had not done.

But Charles Bayne found himself in the same professional dilemma as he had when working for Sir Charles Crosthwaite and courting George Hodgkinson's sister. He supported what Donald Smeaton was trying to do, though he would have tried to moderate his more extreme measures and his aggressive manner. But as Revenue Secretary he was part of Frederic Fryer's personal staff and owed complete loyalty to him. At the last resort he had to accept Fryer's judgement and issue over his own signature what Fryer wanted to say, even where he disagreed with it. With his diplomacy and even temper, he was able to stay on good terms with both men, but he was not able to resolve their differences over policy. Later in his career he would become directly responsible for this issue, as Chapter 10 will record.

Managing the Teak Forests

In the 1890s Burma's second largest export, after rice, was teak. Sales from government forests and royalties from timber concessions also contributed to provincial government revenue. Charles Bayne, as Revenue Secretary, had responsibility for the management and exploitation of the teak forests and for supervising the Burma Forest Department. This was staffed from the Indian Government's forestry service and was under four conservators, each responsible for a separate area of Burma.

The conservators did not always agree and, as no chief conservator was appointed till 1906, this created some friction. As John Nisbet, one of the conservators, wrote in 1901:

'For all matters concerned with questions of general administrative policy, forest settlements, contracts, finance, and matters of routine, the Revenue Secretary exercises an effective control over the four conservators; but he is no more qualified to criticise or to advise the Lieutenant Governor on purely professional matters concerned with scientific forestry and technical questions than he would be to scrutinise and report on engineering projects submitted by the Public Works Department.'

Charles Bayne's coordinating role was thus not a simple one. But he had more direct responsibility for forests than for rice and managed some clear achievements during his tenure as Revenue Secretary.

British policy was gradually to create forest reserves, wholly controlled by government. By 1901 these reserve forests covered 18,000 square miles, though they were only a small fraction of the Burmese forests. But teak trees, wherever they grew, could only be felled if they were selected and 'girdled' by a government forest officer. Girdling, ie cutting round the bark low on the tree, caused the tree to die and it would then be left standing for three years to season before being felled. It might then take another year or more before the timber could be floated down rivers to the ports at Rangoon or Moulmein.

There timber from reserve forests was sold through periodic government auctions.

Outside reserve forests the felling was done by British companies under purchase contracts, especially by the Bombay-Burma Trading Corporation whose activities had provoked the third Burmese war. The company had had its contracts renewed by the provincial government in 1886. It got very favourable rates of royalty and was exempt from having forest officers select its trees for felling, though they still had to be girdled and seasoned in advance. The government was at pains in the 1890s to prevent the Bombay-Burma Trading Corporation from obtaining a monopoly. They not only encouraged other companies, such as Macgregor and Co, to bid for the teak extracted from government forests, but offered them purchase contracts in parts of Burma not covered by the Corporation.

In 1898 a serious crisis broke out with the Bombay-Burma Trading Corporation. Sir Frederic Fryer wrote to Lord Elgin on 10 June: 'The Corporation have been felling large numbers of green teak trees for which they are liable to the cancellation of their agreement without any further notice. I have, however, thought it better to call on the Corporation for an explanation before passing orders.' This led to Berthold Ribbentrop, the Inspector-General of Indian Forests, visiting Burma. He knew the teak forests well, as he had earlier served seven years as a forest conservator in Burma.

Fryer came down from Maymyo to Rangoon for a conference, writing in his diary on 21 July: 'Bayne and Ribbentrop came to see me'. He reported to Elgin:

'There is no doubt that the Agents of the Corporation have felled at least 1000 green teak trees. The plan which I think of following is to cancel the Agreement and then renew it subject to payment of a fine or some fresh terms more favourable to government than the present Agreement. Mr Ribbentrop wished to consult the local forest officers. If we cancel the Agreement and do not renew it, the loss to the Corporation will be very heavy, and it is also doubtful whether the Government can work the forests departmentally for want of the necessary establishment.'

Ribbentrop's forest officers claimed – but could not prove – that at least 7000 green teak trees had been felled. When he met Fryer again at Maymyo on 7 August, he agreed with his strategy, with one important modification. Sir Frederic Fryer confronted the manager of the Corporation, who, after some hesitation, agreed to pay a fine in return for getting the agreement renewed. But he reacted against the further condition added by Ribbentrop. As Fryer wrote to Elgin on 6 October:

'In renewing the permission to fell, I inserted a stipulation that any tree to be felled should first be pointed out to a forest officer. The Corporation demurred to this. They said it would delay their operations very greatly and they hoped I would leave the selection of the trees to their European Assistants, who could be trusted. I said I would so strengthen the staff of forest officers that there should be no delay. The fact is that the Corporation's system is vicious. They allow their Assistants a commission on every tree they bring out and this makes it their interest to fell and bring out as many trees, green or otherwise, as they can.'

The Bombay-Burma Trading Corporation had the last word, however, as they had gone over the heads of Fryer and Ribbentrop. Sir Frederic's letter continues: 'On receipt of the Government of India's telegram [of 30 September] saying that the Corporation's representatives in Simla had complained about the harshness of my conditions, I relaxed the one about felling and only stipulated that the Corporation's Assistants should indicate generally to the forest officers the localities in which they proposed to fell.' This still gave the foresters the chance to see which trees the Corporation had selected during the seasoning process before felling, but it was a much weaker restraint and much easier to evade.

Charles Bayne and his colleagues in the Burma Forest Department were not at all satisfied with this outcome, which only confirmed their distrust of the Bombay-Burma Trading Corporation. They took the opportunity to revise and strengthen the current forest legislation. On 30 August Fryer recorded in Maymyo: 'Bayne sent up his forest bill. I could not finish it today.' They also prepared a more ambitious proposal for taking over the future management of Burma's forests, to put before the Viceroy when he visited Burma. On 11 November, soon after he got back to Rangoon, Fryer 'had a lot of work with Bayne', evidently on this subject, as Lord Elgin arrived on the 16th. At some point while Lord Elgin was in Rangoon – probably on 7-9 December, after his return from Upper Burma – the Burmese forests were discussed with the Viceroy with Charles Bayne present.

The outcome is recorded in a letter sent by Lord Elgin to Fryer on 11 December, just before he left Burma from Moulmein. It deserves extensive quotation, as being the longest letter from any Viceroy on a Burmese economic subject over twenty years or more and the only one in which Charles Bayne is mentioned by name. It begins: 'I have read your draft about the Forests and it may help if I state shortly one or two points which strike me.' The draft is identified as 'Proof of Confidential letter from the Revenue Secretary with connected papers re working of forest in Upper Burma', but the document itself is not included in the Elgin papers.

In setting out his points Lord Elgin makes clear his opposition:

'In the first place, although you speak guardedly and throw a good deal on the Forest Department, it seems to me that the net result is a declaration in favour of departmental working. As you know I hold strongly the opposite view and cannot believe the Government of India will desire, or be allowed, to embark on a huge commercial business of this kind.
'Secondly, you have yourself drawn attention to the large increase in the Forest Staff.

'Thirdly, there are some arguments used in the letter which, from what he said the other day, I imagine I may attribute to Mr Bayne, but even from an out-and-out supporter of departmental working they seem to me open to criticism. No doubt the Corporation overstate their case and use threats which are certainly regrettable. But it seems to me an obvious exaggeration that the Corporation can wind up its business without loss. There is an appearance of animus against the Corporation which I do not think you intend.

'Fourthly, it appears to me doubtful policy to do anything that would have the effect of driving out of Burma a strong and wealthy company. The whole cry nowadays is for the introduction of English capital into India. The Corporation did not sit still when they had complaints against King Theebaw and I am sure they will not spare us if they can allege ill-treatment, while they have, I believe, influential supporters at home.

'[Finally] it is inexpedient to disregard the assistance of private enterprise. When the result of government working is to embark on a large scale in a commercial speculation and come into conflict with trade interests, I believe both financially and politically it will end in failure.'

Lord Elgin's arguments have a very contemporary ring, a century later.

It must have been the Forest Department's initiative to expel the Bombay-Burma Trading Corporation and run all the forests themselves. But Charles Bayne was fully committed to it. He was clearly shocked by the predatory policies of the Corporation, which offended the puritan ethos he had absorbed both from his father and from Donald Smeaton. He was more concerned to protect the Burmese forests for the benefit of the local population than to allow the Corporation to maximise their profits. He gave priority to environmental over economic objectives. He and his colleagues saw a better chance of winning over the Viceroy in person, while he was on Burmese soil, than of convincing the bureaucracy in Calcutta. Their bold stroke did not succeed as they had hoped, but their efforts were not all wasted. Though it took several more years to complete it, 'Bayne's forest bill' was finally adopted as the Burma Forest Act 1902. Sections 30 and 31 confirm: 'All standing teak trees wherever situated shall be deemed to be the property of the Government and shall be reserved trees. No person shall cut, girdle, lop or tap any reserved tree except in accordance with rules made by the Local Government.'

December 1898 marked a new high point in Charles Bayne's career, as the first time he took part in a conference with the Viceroy and was noted in his correspondence. The year 1899 began with some predictable changes. In January Lord Elgin handed over to Lord Curzon as Viceroy and Sir Frederic Fryer went to Calcutta to meet him. In February Frank Gates left on furlough, expecting to become Commissioner on his return. Charles Bayne was looking to a similar promotion later in the year. He and Augusta plucked up their courage and invited the Fryers to dinner. On 4 February Sir Frederic's diary records for the first time: 'Dined with the Baynes'. But what happened next was not foreseen. It sent Charles Bayne's career in a new direction that looked highly promising at first sight but, in the end, caused it to unravel.

Plate I
Charles Bayne aged 1, with his mother and brother Ronald, 1862. This is the first known photo of members of the Bayne family, taken in Berlin.

Plate II
Augusta Bayne on her wedding day, 29 January 1890, in Rangoon.

Plate III
Charles Bayne aged 35 in 1896.
This was taken in a Nottingham studio during his long home leave.

Plate IV
Augusta Bayne aged 32 in 1896.
This is a pair with the photo of Charles in Plate III

Plate V.1
(right)
*Charles Bayne with his
son Ronald aged one,
1898. The photo appears
to be taken in the garden
of their house in
Rangoon, No. 14 Halpin
Road.*

Plate V.2
(below)
*Charles Bayne aged 45,
1906. This was taken in
the same Reigate studio
as Plate VI, soon after his
return from Burma.*

Plate VI
Alice, Madge and Ronald Bayne in 1906.
They would be aged 15, 13 and 8.

Plate VII.1: (above)
Charles Bayne (aged 62) with his daughter Madge and granddaughter Jane in 1923.

Plate VII.2: (below)
Charles (aged 72) and Augusta (aged 69) with their grandson Christopher in 1933. This is the last photo of them that survives.

Plate VIII
Charles Bayne as historian. This undated photo is used as the frontispiece to his
book 'Select Cases in the Council of Henry VII'.

Chapter 8

Unexpectedly Chief Secretary

By the end of the 1890s, the administration of Burma had changed fundamentally, as compared with the position when Charles Bayne arrived 20 years before. Thanks to improved communications, by the railway and the telegraph, power moved away from the Deputy Commissioners in the districts and became more centralised in Rangoon. The Secretariat expanded until it began to look more like the apparatus of a modern government (see Table 8.1).

The Chief Secretary – Edward Symes – exercised general supervision and was directly responsible for the political branch, which covered frontier issues and the Shan States, for military and police affairs and for appointments. The Revenue Secretary – Charles Bayne – was responsible for supervising the revenue, forests and financial branches, which included external trade. He worked both to the Lieutenant Governor and to the Financial Commissioner – Donald Smeaton – who had his own Secretary. He was supported by the Director of Land Records and Agriculture, while a new post of Settlement Commissioner was created in 1900. The Secretary – Frank Gates – was responsible for judicial matters, local administration and social policies. Each of the Secretaries had a specified morning in the week for meeting the Lieutenant Governor, reporting on current business and receiving his instructions. The Chief Secretary called on Tuesdays and the Revenue Secretary on Fridays.

Table 8.1.   The Government of British Burma, January 1899

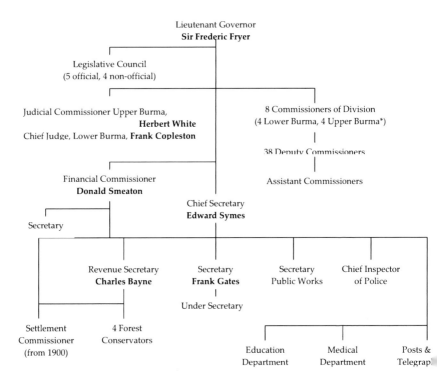

Lieutenant Governor
Sir Frederic Fryer

Legislative Council
(5 official, 4 non-official)

Judicial Commissioner Upper Burma,
Herbert White
Chief Judge, Lower Burma, **Frank Copleston**

8 Commissioners of Division
(4 Lower Burma, 4 Upper Burma*)

38 Deputy Commissioners

Financial Commissioner
Donald Smeaton

Assistant Commissioners

Secretary

Chief Secretary
Edward Symes

Revenue Secretary
Charles Bayne

Secretary
Frank Gates

Secretary
Public Works

Chief Inspector
of Police

Under Secretary

Settlement
Commissioner
(from 1900)

4 Forest
Conservators

Education
Department

Medical
Department

Posts &
Telegraph

* Divisions of Lower Burma: Arakan, Irrawaddy, Pegu, Tenasserim
Divisions of Upper Burma: Mandalay, Meiktila, Minbu, Sagaing

In addition, there were separate Departments for Public Works (with its Secretary), Education, Medical and Posts and Telegraph, whose numbers and importance would grow in the years ahead. A visitor from the University of Chicago in the early 1900s recorded: 'The administrative system of Burma is of the most highly organised type. There is probably no country in the world where every detail of administrative procedure is laid down with greater precision and minuteness.' The responsibility for managing this highly organised system fell directly to Edward Symes as Chief Secretary.

As well as his official duties, Edward Symes led an energetic and outgoing private life, often noted in Frederic Fryer's diary. Though unmarried, he enjoyed female company and arranged 'ladies nights' at Maymyo. He played polo, getting a cut on the head one summer, but he was out riding with the Fryers two days later. He organised a bicycle exhibition at Government House in Rangoon. He built himself a fine house in Maymyo, at great speed. The Fryers had visited the site on 18 March 1898, when Sir Frederic noted in his diary: 'I do not think it will be finished for some time.' But on 30 April 'we all dined with Symes in his new house' and later the Fryers 'went to the improvements Symes had made in his garden'.

Yet all this activity concealed from Fryer that Symes' heavy and unremitting load of work was gradually wearing him down. He had noted in January 1898 that 'Symes is not very well', but he apparently recovered. Fryer did not perceive the signs of severe mental strain that Sir Alexander Mackenzie had noticed back in 1894 and which would have been aggravated by the news of the suicide of his predecessor, George Burgess.

The 'Rangoon Outrage' and Edward Symes' Breakdown

Without warning, Edward Symes broke down on 2 March 1899 and he had to be sent home on leave. Charles Bayne moved up to officiate as Chief Secretary, while Henry Mathews took his place as Revenue Secretary. Fryer reported to Lord Curzon: 'My Chief Secretary, Mr Symes, is very unwell and has had to go home on 3½ months privilege leave. The Revenue Secretary, Mr Bayne, is acting for him, I have a new Revenue Secretary and the Secretary was changed in February, so I have a new Secretariat.' It was as if he was excusing in advance any mistakes made by this inexperienced team. Edward Symes, however, was well enough to dine with the Fryers on 10 March, the evening before his departure. No doubt Sir Frederic and Symes himself expected that three months holiday would restore him to health, while Charles Bayne thought he would only be Chief Secretary for a brief period, as he had been back in 1892.

On 28 March the Lieutenant Governor and Lady Fryer went up to Maymyo, according to custom. Charles Bayne, as Chief Secretary, accompanied them and Augusta came too, presumably with Madge and Ronald. This was their first visit to Maymyo, as far as we know. Boxes of work arrived from Rangoon at intervals, except when, as Fryer records, 'the boxes were thrown off by a pony on Tuesday and all their contents scattered'. But the party had barely left when there was an ugly incident in Rangoon. On the night of 2 April a group of 20 or more soldiers from the West Kent regiment raped a mentally disturbed Burmese woman. The alarm was raised, but by the time the police arrived they could only secure one man, Private Horrocks. The regiment tried to hush the matter up and were loath to cooperate with the police. Horrocks was brought to trial on 10 May, but the court acquitted him, claiming lack of evidence.

Sir Frederic Fryer, isolated in Maymyo, had not thought this worth reporting this to the Viceroy, or even to his diary. This was a serious error, which Edward Symes would surely have corrected, had he been there. But Charles Bayne did not have the experience or authority to put his chief right. Inevitably, the rape got into the Burmese and then the Indian press, so that by 12 June questions were being asked in Parliament in London. Curzon was furious with Fryer for what he regarded as gross negligence over 'the Rangoon outrage' and bombarded with him with telegrams demanding the severest punishment of the culprits. Fryer wrote in his diary on 9 June: 'Viceroy much disturbed about the Horrocks affair. Sent him a long telegram yesterday. I think we ought to have reported the case officially.' He defended himself to Curzon as best he could. 'There was very little excitement among the Burmans and that was why I did not attach political or administrative importance to the occurrence', he wrote. 'It never struck me that that the regimental authorities would fail to use their best exertions to bring the guilty men to justice.' Curzon was not impressed by these feeble excuses and had a low opinion of Fryer from now on.

Both Sir Frederic Fryer and Charles Bayne were greatly relieved that Edward Symes was on his way back from leave, seeming tolerably fit. The Fryers, feeling guilty about their earlier lack of hospitality, 'resolved to ask Baynes to dinner next Monday', so that on 12 June they 'had a farewell dinner party for the Baynes'. Edward Symes got up to Maymyo and resumed his post on 17 June. On the 21st Charles and Augusta left for Minbu, where Charles would be officiating as Commissioner. Minbu was the south-western division of Upper Burma, reached by steamer down the Irrawaddy from Mandalay. It would be an interesting assignment for Charles Bayne, as it included both the ancient ruins of Pagan and the oil wells of Yenaungyang. But he was not destined to undertake it. The day he reached Minbu, on 26 June, he received a telegram from Sir Frederic Fryer recalling him to Maymyo.

In his absence Fryer was 'being horribly bothered about the West Kent case. I do not think we can possibly get anybody convicted.' He sought Edward Symes' advice on how to get the Viceroy off his back and called him in for a conference on 22 June, though two days before he had noted: 'Symes did not look so well today'. As soon as Symes read the file, he would have been appalled at the mess that Fryer and his government was in. He would have understood at once how matters had been mishandled in Rangoon and why the Viceroy was so angry. The reputation of the Burmese administration, that he had built up over so many years, was damaged beyond repair. It was too much for his fragile mental condition. He collapsed once more, far more seriously, and had to be sent home on medical certificate. The doctor reported that his nervous system had completely broken down. He had barely a year to serve before being eligible to retire on pension, but Fryer wondered if he would ever be fit for duty again.

Charles Bayne was therefore called back to become officiating Chief Secretary again for an indefinite future. He met Fryer briefly in Mandalay on 2 July, as the Lieutenant Governor set off on a tour down the Irrawaddy, and is next heard of in Rangoon a month later playing four sets of tennis at Government House. Fryers and Baynes migrated back to Maymyo in mid-August and stayed there till early November, while other members of the Secretariat paid shorter visits. Charles Bayne's time was spent preparing boxes for Fryer during the day and playing tennis with him after office hours. Sometimes Augusta joined the tennis parties or Sir Frederic took her for a drive. Fryer, a frequent player of whist, experimented with bridge, but 'did not much care for the game'.

As Chief Secretary, Charles Bayne became responsible for subjects he had never handled before. He became head of the Political Department, which brought him into operational contact with George Scott, a picturesque figure who had spent much of the last 15 years bringing order to the Shan States of Eastern Burma. In the mid-1890s he had defined the Burma-Siam border. He was now leading the Boundary Commission conducting a similar operation on the Burma-China border, working in difficult country among wild and volatile tribes and negotiating with unpredictable Chinese officials. George Scott emerged from the jungle to reach Maymyo on 22 August, suffering from dysentery. Rather than go to the Fryers, he preferred to have Charles and Augusta look after him till he was fit enough to travel on to Rangoon. Meanwhile the new Revenue Secretary, Henry Mathews, came up to Maymyo to pursue issues that Charles Bayne knew rather better. In September Fryer, Mathews and two of the forest conservators 'decided the terms which may be offered to the Bombay-Burma Trading Corporation'. In October Fryer 'finished the Forest Bill and sent it off', presumably to be looked at in Calcutta.

But the most serious problem remained 'the Rangoon outrage'. In September, while Fryer was holed up in Maymyo, cases were brought against six more soldiers. They were all dismissed by the judge because of unreliable evidence. This increased Curzon's anger. As his first biographer, Lord Ronaldsay, wrote:

> 'Lord Curzon was determined, not only that the offenders should suffer the punishment that they deserved, but that it should be made manifest to the world that official laxity in bringing to account persons guilty of offences against the people of the land would not be tolerated'.

All the soldiers involved were dismissed the army; the West Kent's senior officers were relieved of their commands; and the regiment was banished to Aden for two years, with all leave stopped. In addition, four civil officers in Rangoon were censured for what Curzon called 'extraordinary and reprehensible apathy'. Privately he sent Fryer a series of fiercely critical letters condemning the 'laxity' of his administration, saying on 17 November that his officials 'might have behaved differently had a more vigorous initiative been set to them from headquarters'. It was hard for Fryer to endure this direct rebuke, just at the moment he received the news that his elder son Frank, an army captain, had been killed by a sniper in the early weeks of the Boer War.

As 1900 began, Edward Symes applied for another year's sick leave, doubting whether he would ever be able to return. Both Sir Charles Bernard and Sir Charles Crosthwaite tried to visit him, but were told that 'it upset him greatly to see old friends'. Sir Frederic Fryer, however, successfully put his name in for the KCIE (Knight Commander of the Indian Empire), the fourth time he had been recommended. Meanwhile Charles Bayne continued as Chief Secretary, with regular sessions of tennis at Government House. The Legislative Council held two meetings and passed the Rangoon Waterworks Bill. In February Charles Bayne accompanied Fryer on an official tour of Tenasserim division, probably his first visit to the 'tail' of Burma. They went as far South as Mergui, where they visited a new rubber plantation. On 1 March, before the move to Maymyo, Charles and Augusta escaped for three months privilege leave. Frank Gates, just back from furlough, officiated for Charles. The Baynes would have gone back to England to be briefly reunited with Alice and probably to leave Madge also with her aunt Lydia, as she was now six years old.

During their absence the tense and dangerous situation on the frontier with China dominated Fryer's letters to Curzon. A party of some 500 Chinese marauders crossed the border between Bhamo and Myitkina in the North and had to be turned back by the Burmese military police, leaving 70 dead. Then came reports that up to 7,500 Chinese troops were massing across the border at the same point, though later they withdrew. George Scott reached deadlock with the Chinese boundary commissioners and broke off negotiations, leaving part of the frontier still disputed. When the Baynes returned to Maymyo in mid-June they found George Scott had just arrived and the decision was taken that he should go to Simla to report to the Viceroy. Meanwhile Fryer had learnt that the French intended to send troops from Tonkin into China, to rescue one of their consuls and profit from the confusion leading up to the Boxer Rebellion. He wrote to Curzon suggesting a British force should also invade China from Burma, to secure the border regions and see off any French infiltration.

Curzon gave short shrift to Fryer's proposal, pointing out the folly of invading China when British forces, including many units from India, were tied up in South Africa. His advice was to regard the Burma-China border as running where we thought it did; the Chinese authorities were in no position to contest this and we had no need to occupy the frontier region. 'We are at war with China', he wrote, 'and when peace is restored we shall, I imagine, be at liberty, as part of the conditions, to take what frontier we like.' Charles Bayne shared this view – in 1902 he wrote that the border country was 'inaccessible, inhospitable and unexplored and is inhabited by wild tribes who would resist intrusion into their territory'. Both governments were content to be inactive and China took six years to reply to a British diplomatic note of 1899. Meanwhile George Scott was rewarded with the KCIE.

The agricultural problems that concerned Charles Bayne as Revenue Secretary did not go away. Donald Smeaton was still on the Viceroy's Legislative Council and spending long periods in Calcutta. Curzon himself approved of Smeaton at this stage, saying: 'He is an active pushing man and, I daresay, advertises Burma as effectively as anyone else would do'. Fryer was happy to keep Smeaton out of Burma and recommended his renewal in the post, while admitting to Curzon that the two of them disagreed on tenancies and other land revenue issues. In Smeaton's absence, Fryer was prepared to exert himself over legislation to protect tenants.

He wrote to Curzon in October: 'I have at last succeeded in drafting a tenancy bill. The main object of the bill is to prevent the growth of evils which it may be difficult to remove in future.' The Burma Tenancy Bill of 1900 was more modest than its predecessors and dealt only with security for tenants paying fair rents. But it was criticised by Calcutta for not protecting the landlords' interests. David Norton, who was officiating as Financial Commissioner, was not a forceful character and nothing was achieved.

The Death of Edward Symes

The year 1900 ended quietly with the Fryers playing frequent sessions of tennis with the Baynes, at Maymyo up to mid-November and then at Government House, and occasionally inviting them to dinner. Fryer's nervousness was greatly eased when his surviving son Arthur, also serving with the army in South Africa, was posted to join his parents in Burma. But Charles Bayne was feeling the strain and Fryer agreed that he could go on furlough once Edward Symes was back.

On 6 January 1901 Sir Frederic Fryer wrote to Lord Curzon and his letter contained bad news:

'Sir Edward Symes returned to duty on the 31st of December and took new charge as Chief Secretary next day. He was certified fit for duty by his medical adviser at home. He told me he was still too unwell to work but I persuaded him to stay. The result is that he has broken down again and is in a very nervous and depressed state. He has a little over ten months to serve for his pension so I hope to be able to find some light work for him to do for that period and then he must retire. I am inclined to doubt whether he will ever be fit for any important post again. It is very sad to see a man who was intellectually everything almost imbecile. His work of late years has not been exceptionally heavy and I think his collapse might be due to other causes.'

The next day, 7 January, the Fryers 'dined with the Baynes – got home fairly early.' They must all have been deeply worried about Symes.

But on the 10th Sir Frederic had to write to Lord Curzon again, at greater length, and his letter follows, given almost in full:

'Sir Edward Symes died in hospital at 8.25 am this morning. He returned from sick leave on the 31st of December and on [Tuesday] January 1st told me he was too ill to work. I offered to transfer him to a Commissionership but he said if he could not do the work of Chief Secretary to which he was accustomed he could not do that of a Commissioner as he had not been in charge of a division since 1890. He went to office on Wednesday and did a little work and on Thursday he did a good deal more work. On Friday he said he could not go to office at all and on Saturday he brought me his resignation and said he placed himself entirely in my hands as to what he should do. After some deliberation I proposed to him that he should go to Myingyan, where the Deputy Commissioner is a great friend of his, as Assistant Commissioner. His friends thought that if he had some light work to do he might gradually recover his mental equilibrium.

On Sunday he came to see me again and said he ought to be dismissed for absenting himself from office on Friday. I said this was absurd and tried to get out of him whether he would like to go to Myingyan or would sooner be placed on some other duty. He was very averse to retiring on an invalid pension and I was a little doubtful whether he could be given one, as he had been certified fit for duty by two medical practitioners at Nottingham where he had been living with his brother. I could get nothing out of him so he went away with his friend Mr Fox, Judge of the Chief Court, with whom he was living. On any matters not personally concerning himself he was perfectly rational. On Monday Mr Fox wrote to say that the sooner he was given some light work to occupy his attention the better so I wrote an order on Tuesday transferring him to Myingyan but had not issued it when I heard that he had attempted to commit suicide.

He went out in a cab at 2pm and drove to a shop where he bought a revolver with which he shot himself in the cab. He placed the revolver in his mouth but the shot passed out through the skull above the nose without impacting the brain. I went to the hospital yesterday and the doctors said the wound was not necessarily fatal though they feared complications. I was just getting into my carriage to go to the hospital again this morning when I was informed by telephone that he had just died. It seems that haemorrhage set in and caused his death. I am told that there was a tendency to insanity in his family. The whole story is most pitiful.'

Why did Sir Edward Symes kill himself? Fryer discounts pressure of work and attributes his collapse to unexplained 'other causes'. A hundred years on, an unmarried man like Symes is assumed to be homosexual, but this seems unlikely. There was no breath of scandal and ICS officers often married late or not at all. If Fryer had suspected Symes was gay his attitude would have been much more hostile. When he learnt that Sir Hector Macdonald had shot himself after a homosexual scandal, he commented in his diary: 'Best thing he could do'. What in fact drove Symes over the edge was Fryer's insistence that he return to work, if necessary at a junior level. On three separate occasions Symes had made clear that he was in no state for work: on 1 January when he said he was unfit; on 5 January (Saturday) when he resigned his post; and on 6 January (Sunday) when he invited Fryer to dismiss him. But every time Fryer ignored him, being more concerned about Symes' pension prospects and listening to advice from friends who had also misread the signs.

Fryer's statement that Symes' work 'had not been exceptionally heavy' shows how far he had lost touch with the demands of administering the province. Edward Symes made it look easy, but only at the cost of concealing from others the growing strain upon him. All those who had served with Symes were deeply affected by his fate. Sir Charles Bernard wrote to Herbert White, who was on two years furlough: 'The sad tidings about Symes was a great shock to my wife and me. We were much attached to him. It was a terrible end to so (seemingly) happy a career. If he had managed to marry happily, things might have been very different. A good wife is a strong antiseptic against evil humours'. Sir Charles Crosthwaite (now on the India Office Council in London) thought Symes would have made a worthy Lieutenant Governor, if he had lived. With Edward Symes' death, the quartet – Symes, Smeaton, White and Bayne – that had run Burma together since the early 1880s began to break up.

Chapter 9

The Departure of Smeaton and Fryer

Despite Sir Edward Symes' suicide, the work of governing the province had to go on. Charles Bayne was immediately confirmed as Chief Secretary, but it was a most inauspicious promotion for him. Sir Frederic Fryer left on an official tour of Arakan division. But he cut this short on learning of Queen Victoria's death on 22 January 1901 and returned to Rangoon.

Charles Bayne's Breakdown

On 3 February he had more bad news to report to Lord Curzon:

'In my last letter I gave you an account of the melancholy end of Sir Edward Symes. Yesterday Mr Bayne, who was officiating as Chief Secretary in the absence of Sir E. Symes on leave and who was confirmed in the appointment on the death of Sir E. Symes, broke down in his turn. The Civil Surgeon says he must do no work whatever.

The death of Sir E. Symes was a great shock to Mr Bayne and he has it seems been brooding over it and anticipating a breakdown for himself and now it has come. I heard that Mr Bayne was anxious about himself and asked him when he came to see me last Tuesday whether he found his work too much for him. He said no and that he was quite well. He was to have gone on furlough when Sir E Symes came back but I asked him to stay on till February 20th to which he agreed. The Accountant General wrote to him yesterday and said that it was doubtful whether he could get furlough under the new resolution of January 25th, as he only returned from privilege leave in June last. This seems to have driven him into a state of despondency as he felt sure that he could not continue to carry on the work of Chief Secretary for another year.

I went to see him this morning and said that of course I would keep my word and let him go and he seemed more cheerful when I left. The work of Chief Secretary is hard and continuous but it is nothing like so heavy as it was for the first years after annexation and I cannot understand why it should break men down in this way. I have telephoned to Mr Twomey to come down from Mandalay and take over the post of Chief Secretary but he cannot arrive before Wednesday and will be new to the work so I shall have to do most of it myself for a short time.'

Dreading another suicide, Fryer went to see Charles Bayne three days running, as his diary records. On 3 February he writes: 'Bayne I think is better'; on the 4th: 'Bayne is much better'; on the 5th: 'Bayne is getting alright'. On the next day Daniel Twomey, who would officiate for him, reached Rangoon and on the day after his furlough was authorised by Calcutta. (The Accountant-General – an official of the Indian government seconded to Rangoon – had claimed that ICS officers had to serve at least 18 months between privilege leave and furlough, so that Charles Bayne should have stayed till the end of the year. But Fryer successfully overrode this.) On 8 February there was a setback when 'Bayne fainted in office', before handing over formally to Twomey in the 9th. Even so, Fryer claimed in a letter to Herbert White 'I managed to restore Bayne to his natural state of equanimity'. He could report to Curzon on 14 February: 'Mr Bayne, Chief Secretary, is much better. He attended the meeting of the Legislative Council today. It seems to me strange that the death of Sir E. Symes should have affected him so much.'

In fact, it does not seem strange at all. Charles Bayne had been Edward Symes' closest colleague almost continuously for 15 years and his suicide must have had a traumatic effect. He may never have realised the strain Symes was under and therefore blamed himself, however unreasonably, for not preventing his tragic death. It is also likely that, while Charles Bayne was confident in a supporting role like Revenue Secretary, he was uneasy in the top post in the Secretariat. He had unhappy memories of his first spell officiating as Chief Secretary, back in 1892 when Sir Alexander Mackenzie's wife died. He had not forgotten the humiliation that followed the Rangoon outrage, which took place so soon after he began officiating as Chief Secretary in 1899, following Symes' first collapse. He dreaded a direct meeting with Curzon, who would visit Burma later in the year. All this would have contributed to his breakdown when it looked as if he could not get away on leave.

Charles Bayne, with Augusta and Ronald, sailed for home on 16 February and stayed away for ten months. They spent some time with their daughters Alice and Madge, who were living with Augusta's sister Lydia; there is a photo of Ronald dated 1901 from a Nottingham studio. But Charles Bayne probably immersed himself for the first time in the meticulous historical research, in the Public Record Office, the British Museum and other libraries, that so absorbed him during his retirement. This activity, which gave him intellectual exercise without unwelcome responsibility, would have been an excellent therapy for the accumulated stress of 15 years in the Secretariat and the trauma of Edward Symes' suicide.

In Charles Bayne's absence Fryer and Twomey moved up to Maymyo as usual on 4 April. They were much taken up with preparing for the visit from Lord and Lady Curzon later in the year. Fryer also had to defend himself against long complaints from the Viceroy about persistent 'laxities' in the administration of Burma and the failure to punish them when they occurred. Curzon was particularly fussed about ICS officers who took Burmese wives and mistresses and worried that he might meet them on his visit. But Fryer still found time to recommend Charles Bayne to be Companion of the Star of India (CSI), saying 'Mr Bayne is a very able and hardworking officer and I think his services deserve recognition'. The award came through in November, just as Charles Bayne was leaving England, and Sir Charles Crosthwaite thought it was well earned.

Lord Curzon entered Burma on 21 November, across the land border with Assam, and travelled south to Mandalay, where Lady Curzon met him. The Viceregal party took the train up to Maymyo for a durbar with the Shan princes and then went by steamer down the Irrawaddy. In additional to formal ceremonies, the Curzons were enthusiastic tourists, making a four-hour visit to pagodas and the royal palace in Mandalay, which Fryer found very tiring. Lord Curzon was delighted with what he saw of Burmese culture, though very critical of the way the provincial government had converted part of the palace to offices. By 9 December the party had reached Rangoon. In addition to the usual balls and dinners, Lord Curzon spent three hours at the Shwedagon pagoda. Finally, on 15 December, the Curzons left from Moulmein and Sir Frederic Fryer saw the Viceroy off with great relief. The very next day Charles Bayne came to call on his return to Rangoon – he had clearly played no part in the Viceregal visit and kept out of the way till Curzon had left. He took up his duties again as Chief Secretary and attended two meetings of the Legislative Council, to which he was reappointed. But Fryer did not think he looked very much better for his trip home.

Donald Smeaton's Resignation

Sir Frederic Fryer was due to retire in early 1902. Donald Smeaton considered that he was the best qualified man to succeed him and he was in fact the only eligible candidate from the Burma Commission. As well as being Financial Commissioner, he had been a member of the Viceroy's Legislative Council since 1898. He had spent much of his time since then in Calcutta, hoping to influence Lord Curzon and his Executive Council to back his appointment as Lieutenant Governor. But as they steamed down the Irrawaddy, Curzon and Fryer had discussed the choice of his successor. Curzon wrote to Fryer on 9 January 1902: 'You strongly advised me against appointing Mr Smeaton and said you thought the interests of the province would best be served, in the absence of any suitable local candidate, by the appointment of an outsider as the next Lieutenant Governor.' Fryer confirmed his hostility to Smeaton, writing: 'Mr Smeaton is by no means popular in Burma, whatever his friends in the press may say to the contrary'.

Curzon's preferred outside candidate was Sir Hugh Barnes, his Foreign Secretary, who had no Burmese experience. However, he had appointed Barnes as President of the Central Committee of the Delhi Durbar to be held early in 1903. So Fryer had to agree to Curzon's request that he stay on an extra year till Barnes could be released. As Sir Charles Crosthwaite commented to Herbert White, now back in Rangoon as Chief Judge of the Chief Court: 'Fryer is to have an extension, not because he has done well (I don't think anyone thinks he has done justice to the appointment) but because the man Curzon has chosen cannot be sent at once'.

Curzon bluntly informed Donald Smeaton that he would not get the post. Smeaton was furious at being passed over and was convinced that Curzon was personally responsible. He whipped up a hostile campaign against Curzon in the press, resigned from the ICS and returned to London to pursue his vendetta, in the most intemperate language. Curzon wrote to Fryer on 21 February: 'When Smeaton was not made Lieutenant Governor, he and his friends raised a howl and nothing could exceed the bitterness of the former towards myself'. He added on 10 April: 'The Smeatons have departed, leaving a trail of calumny on myself behind them.' Fryer responded: 'He is a very extraordinary and unreliable person and I am quite certain that if he had succeeded me, the government would soon have seen cause to regret it. He is eaten up with conceit and has no common sense.' But Sir Charles Crosthwaite in London thought both sides were at fault. He wrote to White: 'I cannot help being sorry for Smeaton, though

I think the Viceroy is right. But he might have done it nicely. Smeaton has been very mad over it. I fear he will not get over the blow to his self-esteem'.

Donald Smeaton, like Edward Symes, revealed mental instability, though in a more obvious way. He quarrelled with everyone, in particular his superiors, like Crosthwaite and Fryer. This in the end was his undoing. But though Sir Charles Crosthwaite had earlier called him 'crazy', he recognised his merits as an administrator. He commended him to Lord Elgin as being 'as good an authority as anyone alive on the Land Revenue of Burma. I do not know anyone of greater energy and ability in the Civil Service.' Sir Alexander Mackenzie also thought highly of him. When recommending him for the CSI in 1895 he told Lord Elgin: 'Mr Smeaton has done a great work in Burma in organising and improving its Revenue System. His work is extremely heavy and he never spares himself. He is a man of marked ability.'

Sir Alexander Mackenzie added 'he has toned down the tendency to impetuosity which created a little prejudice against him some years ago' – but here he was wrong. Donald Smeaton took a delight in advancing unorthodox views and in criticising the conventional wisdom. He thought that the suppression of the monarchy and the annexation of Upper Burma were ill-judged decisions. He disagreed with the imposition on the Burmese of administrative structures from outside. He identified early on the problems affecting rice farmers and advocated measures to deter the alienation of land and to protect tenants. His ideas often went against the position adopted by the government, either in Rangoon or Calcutta, but later events would show that he was right and they were wrong. Charles Bayne had sympathy with many of his views, which had been shared by George Hodgkinson, and supported his efforts to improve conditions for Burmese cultivators. So he would have been sorry to see him disappointed at the end. Donald Smeaton was the second member of the quartet to go; now only White and Bayne remained.

The Delhi Durbar

Throughout 1902 Sir Frederic Fryer made Charles Bayne stay on as his Chief Secretary, though Fryer seemed to be marking time till his departure. Charles Bayne resumed his sessions of tennis at Government House and on 13 February the Fryers 'dined with the Baynes – there was a party of ten.' There was the usual migration to Maymyo, from 24 March to 20 November, where Charles and Augusta were more socially active than before. In addition to having Charles Bayne at their own tennis parties, the Fryers several times 'went to tennis at Bayne's.' On 1 September the Fryers 'had Mr and Mrs Bayne to dinner and played bridge'. This may have been Augusta's initiative – separate evidence suggests Charles was a reluctant player.

Sir Frederic Fryer still had to defend himself against periodic broadsides from Curzon. One such attack arose over the choice of a new Financial Commissioner to succeed Donald Smeaton. Curzon reported on 11 May that the Revenue and Administration members of his Council were very critical of Burma's performance in this field; they had suggested another outside appointment. 'I know this will produce a howl of rage from Burma', he wrote. 'But as Burma is always howling, I suppose an addition to the volume should be discounted.' Fryer admitted on 19 May that David Norton, who had officiated for Smeaton, had been rather idle and could not be confirmed in the post. But he strongly rejected the attacks on Burma's revenue work. 'I am somewhat staggered [at what is] thought of our revenue work. The Revenue and Administrative Department never passed any orders without sufficient knowledge – I thought the defect on the other side.' He recommended William Hall as the new Financial Commissioner, whom Curzon accepted. Charles Bayne knew him well; they had first met at Myanaung in 1884, when Hall was Settlement Officer, and he had since been Director of Land Records under Crosthwaite. In October Curzon again took Fryer to task on the standards of his administration, claiming that he should never have defended Hugh McColl, an officer with a Burmese wife. To answer 'HE's very disagreeable letter', Fryer relied on defensive material rapidly assembled from the files by Charles Bayne; his note still survives in Fryer's papers.

The Delhi Durbar provided some relief from the routine. This brought to Delhi delegations from all over British India for ceremonies lasting from 29 December 1902 to 4 January 1903. Sir George Scott was there, bear-leading a group of princes from the Shan States, and gives a vivid account in his published diaries; though just as laconic as Fryer's, they are more entertaining. Scott brought his charges by rail to Rangoon on the morning of 17 December, 'met Thirkell White and Bayne' and next day boarded the steamer for Calcutta. The Lieutenant Governor's party left Rangoon a few days later. The delegation included: Sir Frederic and Lady Fryer with their son Arthur, who acted as private secretary; Herbert Thirkell White, now Chief Judge of the Chief Court in Rangoon, with his wife Fanny; James Lowis, the Government Advocate; Henry Todd Naylor, a divisional Commissioner; and Charles Bayne, the Chief Secretary, with Augusta.

When they all met again on the train from Calcutta to Delhi, Sir George Scott writes 'Bayne brought with him my new uniform, which had not been ready when I left Rangoon. Thirkell White, Todd Naylor, Lowis and I played bridge all day on the train'. This was a friendly action by Charles Bayne, while Herbert White was certainly the moving spirit behind the bridge game – he wrote a book on bridge in his retirement. The train reached Delhi on 27 December and that evening Scott 'took in Mrs Thirkell White to dinner; as lively and charming as usual'. Scott was then busy settling in his princes and making calls, but on 30 December 'after dinner I was roped in to play bridge with the Thirkell Whites and Baynes.' Since Charles Bayne had not been part of the bridge party on the train, the implication is that Augusta liked to play bridge while he did not; Scott was needed to make up a four. Two days later, on 1 January 1903, Scott 'at dinner took in Mrs Bayne, who had a lot of conversation.'

Amid all the Durbar festivities, Charles Bayne still had work to do as head of the Burma Political Department. Sir George Scott records on 3 January: 'Did a memo for Bayne on extra-territoriality in Siam'. This must refer to the problem of Shan princes claiming lands beyond the Siamese border; it is not clear if Charles Bayne asked for the memo or Scott volunteered it. A day later (4 January) Scott was lobbied by one of his princes in great distress because he did not get a nine-gun salute, as other chiefs had done. He records: 'It is a shame. Saw Bayne about it at dinner. [He] promised to put it before Barnes, who is to see the L. G. tomorrow.' Charles Bayne's intervention had an effect, though it was delayed by nine months. By that time Sir Hugh Barnes was himself the Lieutenant Governor.

A sympathetic picture of the Baynes emerges from Sir George Scott's diary. Scott was an unorthodox operator, who often crossed swords with officials at headquarters, but he clearly liked and trusted Charles Bayne. For his part, Charles Bayne showed himself both a helpful friend and a conscientious colleague, with meticulous attention to detail. Augusta was obviously an active support to him, with social gifts that made up for his more retiring nature.

Back in Rangoon after the Durbar, Sir Frederic Fryer went through a prolonged series of farewell ceremonies in the spring of 1903. He still found time for games of tennis with Charles Bayne, who sometimes won. Fryer's diary for 27 March records: 'Played tennis – White and I against A [Fryer's son Arthur] and Bayne. The latter were too strong for us'. Finally, on 4 April, Fryer handed over to Sir Hugh Barnes as Lieutenant Governor and sailed from Rangoon that afternoon.

Sir Frederic Fryer had been Chief Commissioner and Lieutenant Governor of Burma for ten years – from 1892 through to 1903, with only a short break when Sir Alexander Mackenzie returned. He had begun well, assuming authority easily and developing a system of regular tours around the province. He impressed Lord Lansdowne and Lord Elgin in his early years and they rewarded him by confirming him as Chief Commissioner, awarding him the KCSI and promoting him to Lieutenant Governor. But the longer he stayed, the more he became a prisoner of routine, reluctant to admit new ideas and slow to respond to the changing needs of his administration. His practice of spending half the year in Maymyo, from 1897 onwards, cut him off from the business of government and led to some major lapses of judgement, especially over the Rangoon rape case. So over time his reputation fell quite low. Herbert White, who praises Bernard, Crosthwaite and Mackenzie in his memoirs, passes over Fryer in silence. Sir Charles Crosthwaite thought Fryer had wasted his chances and records how he was notorious among other ICS members for his 'insouciance'. Lord Curzon, who never forgot the 'Rangoon outrage', thought Fryer 'an easy-going, lethargic, played-out sort of man.' It was a cruel judgement, but sadly accurate by the end.

Chapter 10

Financial Commissioner and Leaving Burma

When Sir Hugh Barnes took over as Lieutenant Governor, Lord Curzon lost no time in warning him of the low standards prevailing in the Burmese administration, which he would have to correct. In many cases, Curzon wrote on 16 June 1903:

> 'I have been forcibly impressed by the shocking drafting of the Burma Secretariat – indiscreet, careless and slipshod. You will have to introduce a higher standard in this respect. Another point that struck me forcibly during the Fryer regime and about which I frequently spoke and corresponded with him was the prevalent laxity both in the conduct of officials in Burma and in the official treatment of their delinquencies.'

Sir Hugh Barnes had worked with Curzon for three years and, unlike Sir Frederic Fryer, he knew how to handle him. It was fruitless to argue over drafting standards, though the attacks would have been deeply wounding to Charles Bayne. Curzon often condemned the drafting of proposals when he disagreed with them.

However, Barnes sent back on 18 July a firm rebuttal of laxity, which shows Charles Bayne at work:

> 'I am afraid there is no doubt that the subordinate services in Burma are very corrupt. But I have not found the Secretariat at all inclined to be lax in dealing with them. I think I have hardly passed a week in Burma without being asked to

suspend, reduce, dismiss or pass over some *Myook*, clerk, forest ranger or provincial service officer and, when cases of promotion come before me, it is astonishing the number of men whose promotion has been deferred or whom I have to pass over for some delinquency or other. Mr Bayne, the Chief Secretary, is a very able man and very thorough in dealing with cases of this kind.'

Leave on Medical Certificate

Sir Hugh Barnes was a more intelligent and sensitive chief than Sir Frederic Fryer. Before long he perceived that the strain of his office was again pushing Charles Bayne to the edge of collapse. In August he sent him home on leave on medical certificate and his report to Curzon, on 5 September, speaks for itself:

'I am sorry to say I have had the misfortune to lose my Chief Secretary, Mr Bayne, a very able and a very sound man with 17 years' experience of this Secretariat. I was obliged to let him go as he was in imminent danger of breaking down and I think the recollection of the fate of his two predecessors Sir Edward Symes and Mr Burgess, both of whom committed suicide, was beginning to tell on his nerves. He is a great loss. I am taking Mr Gates, Commissioner of Meiktila, in his place.'

Sir Hugh Barnes continued with a general comment:

'All officers in Burma are certainly very hard worked; I do not quite know why it should be. Sir C. Crosthwaite is reported to have said that the North-West Provinces were child's play after Burma, even as it was in his time. Certainly the amount of detail to be got through is very great. Mines, oilfields, seaports, forests and military police give us a lot of work from which many provinces are free. We also have a frontier and our full share of political work with all the Shan states. Also the principles of our land revenue and excise (opium) administration are still in a fluid state and we administer Upper Burma with what seems to me, after my frontier experience, an unnecessary amount of minute legal detail.'

Curzon, who had never reacted to Edward Symes' suicide, was moved to respond on 20 September:

'It is unfortunate that three Chief Secretaries in succession have broken down. The strain upon them must be unduly heavy. As you say, the peculiar characteristics of the province, both frontier and inland, administrative, industrial and commercial, combine to generate a series of problems that are seldom united in the same area. Moreover, part of the province is still young and has hardly settled down to the traditions of British administration.'

Sir Charles Crosthwaite still kept a paternal eye on his former staff from Burma. 'I heard Bayne was coming home but did not know he had arrived,' he wrote to Herbert White in October. 'I am glad he has come and hope he will take a long rest.' It was soon clear that he would not return to Rangoon as Chief Secretary. Frank Gates was confirmed in the post on 20 September, while Charles Bayne was promoted to Commissioner the same day. He could have had few happy memories of his time as Chief Secretary. But he had survived, without ruining his health like George Burgess or breaking down completely under the strain like Edward Symes.

For the next 12 months he and his family were back in England and he would have picked up his historical researches so as to restore his mental equilibrium. There was also time spent with Augusta's family and Ronald was photographed in the same Nottingham studio as two years earlier. As he was 7 in August 1904, Charles and Augusta would expect to leave him in England with his sisters. But it appears that Aunt Lydia, now nearly 60, could not cope with an active small boy as well as the two girls and there may also have been problems with suitable schools in Nottinghamshire. The upshot was that Augusta remained behind to look after the children and settled on the south coast. Sir Frederic Fryer found her there early in 1905: 'We saw Mrs Bayne not very long ago', he wrote to Herbert White on 5 February. 'She is living at Hastings or St Leonard's – I forget which – but whichever it is, she does not seem to care for it very much.' No doubt she was worried about Charles, who was passed fit for work and had to return to Burma on his own in August 1904.

In Charge of Land and Revenue Administration

Charles Bayne came back to Rangoon just as William Hall, the Financial Commissioner, went off on 15 months' furlough. When Hall returned from leave in December 1905, he was appointed as Burma's representative on the Viceroy's Legislative Council, which required him to spend the winter in Calcutta. So Charles Bayne was appointed officiating Financial Commissioner in his place and held the post for the next 20 months, being also re-appointed to the Burmese Legislative Council. He was extremely well fitted for the post, thanks to his long years handling economic issues in the Secretariat. But now, for the first time, he had greater freedom to expound and promote his own views.

Charles Bayne made an impact as Financial Commissioner in land settlement operations. Settlement officers were active all over the province at this time, revising settlements in Lower Burma and making new ones in Upper Burma, district by district. They would submit their reports to a conference consisting of the Commissioner and Deputy Commissioner for the district concerned, together with the newly created Settlement Commissioner. The Financial Commissioner would then add his comments, before the documents were endorsed by the Lieutenant Governor and remitted to Calcutta.

The reports show Charles Bayne – now without family ties – travelling up Eastern Burma by train in the spring of 1905, commenting on land settlements as he goes. He signed off his comments on the settlement for Hanthawaddy district at Pegu on 22 February; for part of Prome district at Toungoo on 2 March; for part of Tharrawaddy district at Meiktila on 10 March; for Kyaukse district at Kyaukse itself on 14 March; and for Myaungma district at Maymyo on 5 April. He also took the opportunity to inspect the tax offices in the first four places, finding them all in good or fair order. He made a similar journey through Western Burma a year later, by steamer up the Irrawaddy, inspecting tax offices in Bassein, Myaungma, Henzada, Prome, Sagaing and Katha. But by now William Hall was back from his leave and insisted on commenting on land settlements from Calcutta.

Charles Bayne's observations on these five settlement reports show his deep knowledge and interest in different methods of agriculture and their fiscal implications. Kyaukse was the only district in Upper Burma, being on the Irrawaddy just south of Mandalay. Here he commented on the value of irrigation, on the merits of introducing new crops into Upper Burma and the effect of the railway on crop prices. The settlement in Prome district covered an area of poor land, where many people had migrated south to find better farming conditions in the delta. He advised a low tax rate, as the land was so infertile. The other three settlements were from the area of intense rice cultivation in Lower Burma. In Hanthawaddy and Tharawaddy, in the middle delta, he noted the loss suffered by farmers when the river flooded. This should be taken into account in setting tax rates, while experiments in cultivating rice in deep water should be pursued.

In Myaungma, near the river mouth, he advised against trying to determine squatters' title to land at the time of settlement operations. He then noted his anxiety about land tenure, which had concerned him for 15 years or more: 'The policy of the government is to keep the soil in the possession of the actual cultivator and to offer obstacles to the formation of a landlord class. The large increase in the number of tenants is proof of the rapidity in which a permanent tenant class is coming into existence in Lower Burma'. In Myaungma he believed most of the tenants were in a comfortable condition and the bulk of the landlords belonged to the agriculturist class, i.e. were farmers themselves. But in Hanthawaddy he was less confident, as both rents and levels of debt were high: 'Is the position of the tenant strong?' He wanted more data on different types of tenancy: 'I propose to address the Settlement Commissioner separately on this subject.'

Charles Bayne had the misfortune to be responsible for revenue administration during two years of bad harvests. These adverse conditions revealed the worsening plight of the Burmese rice farmers, which he and Donald Smeaton had recognised back in 1891 but no measures had been taken to relieve them. In fact, conditions were even worse than he suspected. For many years revenue and settlement reports had provided comfort to the colonial government by showing most land still in the hands of Burmese cultivators, with tenancies and holdings by 'non-agriculturists', i.e. money-lenders, a minority. But the adverse conditions were beginning to reveal this data to be thoroughly unreliable. In fact absentee landlords were widespread, possessing more than half the land in some districts, while many farmers held their land on one-year tenancies.

The *Report on Land Revenue Administration* for the year ending 30 June 1905 – his first year – recorded: 'The agricultural season was on the whole not very favourable.' Despite this, the acreage under crops exceeded 12.5 million acres, of which 9 million were devoted to rice. Tax collection was difficult: 'The losses of cultivators owing to the unfavourable season necessitated the more frequent resort of headmen to coercive process.' There was also a slump in export demand: 'The general lightness of the crop reduced the surplus paddy available for export. But it is improbable that the cultivators generally reaped any advantage from the market.' Because of cattle disease and floods, 'land was heavily mortgaged to cover losses' and there was a general increase in land being held by absentee landlords and money-lenders. Conditions seemed to be particularly hard in Arakan division, where the Commissioner noted that 'much land has been relinquished; it may be necessary to defer the collection of the revenue.' But Charles Bayne ruled against it: 'The district has no doubt suffered from the bad season but the revenue rates are still light. The Arakanese are notoriously backward with their revenue.'

The 1904-1905 Report contained no proposals to improve the conditions for landowners or tenants. This reflected the position taken by Sir Hugh Barnes; but Barnes was on his way out. Right from his arrival in Burma, he had confessed to his wife that his ambition was to get back to London and a seat on the India Office Council as soon as he could. Early in 1905 Sir Charles Crosthwaite retired after ten years on the Council and Barnes was chosen to fill his place, leaving Burma after just two years. Lord Curzon, now in his last year as Viceroy, appointed Sir Herbert Thirkell White as Lieutenant Governor and he took over in May.

Charles Bayne's second year as Financial Commissioner was even worse for the farmers. *The Report on Land Revenue Administration* for 1905-6 recorded: 'The year under review was not favourable to the agriculturist either in Lower or Upper Burma. The year is a very instructive one as showing what the effects of a bad season can be on the alienation of land in Burma. In the Pyapon District no less than 29 per cent of the occupied land of the district is said to be in the hands of alien money-lenders.' Sales and mortgages of land had increased considerably, with more land passing to absentee landlords: 'These figures compare unfavourably with last year.' Burmese farmers in Arakan division were again in deep difficulty over their taxes, because of competition from more frugal Indians moving in from Chittagong. But Charles Bayne saw his first responsibility as being to ensure that the revenue on which the provincial government relied was collected promptly and in full. As last year, he declared the Arakanese to be 'unduly querulous'. He issued general instructions on speeding up tax returns and ruled that the commissions on tax collection granted to village headmen must inevitably fall when revenue itself fell.

Charles Bayne's Land Alienation Bill

But this year there was at last movement again on legislation to protect the rice farmers. Herbert White was convinced that such legislation was necessary. In his very first letter to Lord Curzon, on 4 June 1905, he wrote: 'I propose to take up the Land Alienation Bill, a matter which I have very much to heart. If we do not get it soon we shall be reproached for lack of foresight'. The Resolution covering the *Report on Land Revenue Administration* for 1905-6 reported that policies intended to keep farmers on the land were having only a limited effect:

'It is clear that other and more direct measures are required if the land is to be retained in the hands of the cultivating classes. A Bill on the lines of the Punjab Land Alienation Act is therefore under consideration. By these means it is hoped to stop the process by which land in Burma has been passing slowly but surely out of the hands of the agricultural classes. It has also been considered desirable to provide for the protection of tenants and a bill for that purpose has been prepared.'

As reported in Chapter 7, there had been no progress in agrarian legislation under Sir Frederic Fryer, largely because of the antagonism between him and Donald Smeaton. When William Hall took over from Smeaton in 1902 he attacked the issue with new vigour and in March 1903, just as Fryer was leaving, he produced a new Land Alienation Bill. But Sir Hugh Barnes was not impressed with this and, after long reflection, sent it back to Hall in July 1904 with a list of critical comments and queries. William Hall had just time to send this round to divisional Commissioners for their reactions, before he went off on furlough and handed the whole dossier to Charles Bayne. The Commissioners were asked to comment by December, but in fact some took till May 1905. When all had commented, Charles Bayne prepared a careful note for Herbert White, dated 26 July 1905 and supported by an amended version of the Bill. This was to be his last major contribution to policy-making.

William Hall's Bill had followed Smeaton's original proposal in making all transfers of land subject to approval by Deputy Commissioners. Charles Bayne challenged this for both economic and administrative reasons. His economic reasons are worth quoting at length:

'The object of the legislation is to protect the cultivator against himself, to prevent him from parting with his land. Free trade in land is not an evil per se. A measure that places obstacles in the way of such free trade must be radically defective. It is the abuse of free trade which is the evil and it is because this abuse is so serious in the case of agriculturists that we propose to deprive them of the right of free transfer. Special reasons exist in Burma which render it undesirable to restrict free trade in land too closely. A large part of Burma is undeveloped and capital is necessary for its development. Any restriction on the alienation of land must diminish its value and must retard the development of the country. We must proceed cautiously.'

Administratively, in Charles Bayne's view, the original Bill would impose intolerable burdens on Deputy Commissioners, who would need to examine each case. He also considered a proposal to allow free land transfers between residents of the same village would have perverse effects, as it could easily be abused by Burman money-lenders and give them an advantage over the Indian Chettyar financiers. Bayne considered the Chettyar had good qualities: he wanted his money back with interest, but preferred not to acquire land unless he had no alternative. If capital was required for Burma's development, he should be encouraged. But the local money-lender worked with a small capital, demanded exorbitant interest and desired to obtain land and become a landlord.

Charles Bayne therefore recommended a simpler measure. Transfers of land between farmers and between those who were not farmers, as well as any purchases of land by farmers, could be conducted freely. Only sales of land from farmer to non-farmer needed to be sanctioned by a Deputy

Commissioner. Charles Bayne recognised that this system would only work with a careful definition of who was a farmer (or 'agriculturist' in the jargon). He supplied such a definition: an agriculturist was a person who engaged personally in agricultural labour and earned his living thereby in whole or part. The definition extended to his wife and other dependants and included pastoral pursuits but did not include persons engaged in money-lending. Finally, Charles Bayne endorsed the limitation of mortgages to those where the borrower enjoyed the benefits of the land and its produce, though he recommended a maximum term of 15 years against the ten years favoured by Hall.

Herbert White took his time to consider these recommendations, but on 17 May 1906 he sent his draft Bill to Calcutta with a long explanatory letter. His Bill adopted all Charles Bayne's ideas, except that it did not offer a precise definition of agriculturist. Calcutta took even longer to digest it, but finally wrote back in October 1907 with various reservations and instructed White to open the Bill to public consultation. This revealed widespread opposition in Burma. It was claimed the bill would reduce the value of land and the area cultivated, thus yielding less tax revenue. Cultivators would be less able to borrow and banks would be ruined, as their lending prospects were reduced. These arguments reflected the views of the expatriate business community represented on the Burmese Legislative Council. The rice traders and millers, who were suffering from a prolonged slump in the export business, were against any measure that might make their lives harder. The financial community were hit by a world-wide credit crunch in 1907, which caused many of them to call in their loans.

Because of this opposition Sir Herbert White was unable to get his measure enacted during his five years in office and the same thing happened to his Tenancy Bill, issued later in 1906. Both bills were abandoned by his successor. White later wrote in *A Civil Servant in Burma*:

'I had much at heart the enactment of legislation for restraining the alienation of land and for the protection of tenants. I have no doubt that gradually but surely the Burman is being squeezed off the land, which will fall into the hands of non-agriculturists and natives of India. From an economic point of view the position is probably sound. More rice will be grown for export; more land revenue and customs duty will be garnered. But there are other considerations. The standard of living will be lowered. The deterioration of the Burmese race which will inevitably accompany the divorce from the land will be subject for regret when it is irremediable.'

Charles Bayne would have agreed. But in fact he had left Burma before White sent his first Bill to Calcutta.

Leaving Burma

When Sir Herbert White took over from Sir Hugh Barnes, Charles Bayne must have considered what his prospects would be for the rest of his career. On the face of it, they looked good. He was still under 45. The new Lieutenant Governor was a close friend and colleague of long standing. William Hall was due to retire early in 1907 and Charles Bayne would be strongly placed to take over from him as Financial Commissioner on a confirmed basis. If that should happen, he could even be a candidate to take over as Lieutenant Governor when Herbert White's term ended. But it did not happen. The post of Financial Commissioner passed instead to Frank Gates, with whom Charles Bayne had shared so many years in the Secretariat. Gates held it till he retired, as Sir Frank Campbell Gates KCIE, in 1914.

Financial Commissioner would have been the post that most attracted Charles Bayne. Family legend says that he retired early because the senior post he wanted went to someone else. Sir Herbert White's letters to Lord Minto in 1906 cover other appointments, but are silent on his recommendations for Financial Commissioner. But if he preferred Gates over

Bayne, for whatever reason, Charles Bayne did not hold it against him and there is evidence suggesting that he had decided not to compete. Immediately after his arrival as Lieutenant Governor in May 1905, Herbert White began urging Lord Curzon to appoint members of the Burma Commission to senior posts in the Indian government in Calcutta, which had never been done before. As suitable candidates he suggested Alan Irwin and Harvey Adamson, both divisional Commissioners, and Frank Gates, his Chief Secretary, 'any of whom is fit for any appointment; Mr Gates is really brilliant'. Charles Bayne's name would surely have been on this list if he had wanted to advance his career. Instead, he must have decided that he no longer wanted to risk the continued strain to his health of high office. He preferred to get back home to his family and resume his hobby of historical research. He took the opportunity now open to him to retire early.

Like all ICS officers, Charles Bayne became entitled to a pension of £1000 a year on completing 25 years, counted from his entry date of September 1880. Of these, 21 years had to be on active service. By May 1906 he satisfied both criteria. On 9 April, when William Hall returned from Calcutta, Charles Bayne handed back the Financial Commissionership to him. He remained at Maymyo 'on special duty' for the next month. Then he came down to Rangoon, resigned from the Legislative Council and left Burma on 10 May. He was granted six months privilege leave and 'leave on private affairs' and was then 'permitted to retire' from the ICS on 10 November 1906. He was the third member of the original quartet – Symes, Smeaton, White and Bayne – whose career had ended prematurely. Sir Herbert White, the Lieutenant Governor and the last survivor of the four, inserted into the *Report on Land Revenue Administration* for 1905-1906 a farewell tribute to his work in Burma: 'Through the retirement of Mr C. G. Bayne, the Province has lost an officer of experience and ability, whose zeal and devotion to the best interests of Burma were unwearying'.

Chapter 11

Early Research: Queen Elizabeth I

Charles Bayne returned to England in the summer of 1906 and was reunited with his family. They passed a few of their early months at the Star and Garter Hotel, Petersham, before moving to a house in Beckenham in the south-east suburbs. There is an attractive photo of the three children, Alice, Madge and Ronald, at this time from a Reigate studio, where Charles also had his picture taken (Plates V.2 and VI). The surviving print shows him now in glasses, but not looking seriously aged as compared with the photo dating from ten years before (Plate III). No doubt it was a great relief to escape from the responsibilities that had weighed on him for so long in Burma.

As soon as he was settled in England, Charles Bayne immersed himself in his historical research and in preparing material for publication. This was his main activity throughout his retirement. He concentrated at first on the early years of the reign of Queen Elizabeth I and the political implications of the religious settlement introduced at the start of her reign. In choosing this precise period and subject he was clearly influenced by the historical work earlier done by his father and his elder brother. Peter Bayne, in his later life, had moved away from strictly religious themes to write a study of the Civil War in Britain. The Rev Ronald Bayne had begun editing a contemporary life of John Fisher, Bishop of Rochester, beheaded under Henry VIII for the same reasons as Thomas More. (In fact only a transcript of the text was ever published.) These influences directed Charles Bayne to the religious changes under the

Tudors and Stuarts, though he chose a different period, so as to produce work that was independent of theirs.

His first years after his return from Burma were extremely productive, which shows that he must already have begun his researches while recovering from his breakdowns in 1901 and 1903-4, if not earlier. His first article, 'The Coronation of Queen Elizabeth', appeared in the *English Historical Review*, volume xxii (October 1907), only 18 months after his return. In the following year he published a double article, 'The First House of Commons of Queen Elizabeth', in the *English Historical Review*, volume xxiii (July and October 1908). There was then a gap of several years, until he brought out two works in 1913. Another article, 'The Visitation of the Province of Canterbury, 1559', came out in the *English Historical Review*, volume xxviii (October 1913). A book, *Anglo-Roman Relations, 1558-1565*, was published by the Clarendon Press, Oxford, as the second volume of Oxford Historical and Literary Studies.

All of these works are distinctive in three ways: by the systematic assembly of a wide range of material to support the narrative or the case being argued; by the close and detailed study of the original texts thus assembled, to extract the maximum evidence from them; and by rigorous, forensic argument, which often challenges accepted scholarly opinion. They are remarkable achievements for a man with no academic background who – as he himself said – finished his formal education at the age of seventeen, when he began his preparation for entry to the ICS.

The Coronation of Elizabeth I

Charles Bayne, in beginning his first article, declares Elizabeth's coronation on 15 January 1559 to be a 'notable event for two reasons'. First, it was 'the last coronation in England with the Latin service of Plantagenet times'. Second, 'the order of the ceremony throws light on the religious opinions which Elizabeth held, or professed to hold, at the beginning of her reign'. To establish exactly what happened at the coronation, he examines the two principal sources, which contradict each other.

One source is an undated account by an unknown English spectator, surviving only in a later copy. The other is a report by an Italian resident in London called Il Schifanoya, writing on 23 January 1559 to the court of Mantua. (A third, shorter account survives in the College of Arms.) 'Recent writers have preferred to base their accounts on the Italian report', he notes, because 'we know when and by whom it was written'. But 'of the English report nothing is known' and so it seemed to have become discredited. Charles Bayne then compares the two reports with the *Liber Regalis*, the service book used for the coronation over three centuries, from 1307 to 1661. This shows that the English report follows accurately the complicated sequence of the ceremony, so that 'we may accept the English report as the production of an eye-witness'. The Italian report proves to be confused and inaccurate – 'it is unable to sustain the test'.

Having restored faith in the English report, Charles Bayne uses it to solve a mystery concerned with the coronation. It appeared that Elizabeth withdrew at one point from the service, because she was displeased that the officiating priest elevated the host. Most historians stated that the Dean of Westminster sang the service. Bayne argues that the dean, George Carew, was a notorious trimmer and would never have done anything to displease the queen. It could be suggested that Elizabeth did not withdraw, or that her withdrawal had no special significance, but 'this view is untenable'. The only possible answer was that the bishop – Oglethorpe of Carlisle – sang the service, as the English report stated, though the dean might have led the introit. On Christmas Day 1558 Bishop Oglethorpe had taken the service before the queen and she had withdrawn because he had elevated the host. Exactly the same thing happened at the coronation. Elizabeth on both occasions disassociated herself from the visible sign of the doctrine of transubstantiation, which was integral to the Roman rites restored by Mary but would not be part of the settlement brought in by Elizabeth.

At the end, Charles Bayne publishes the full texts of the English and Italian reports, together with the shorter account from the College of Arms, with detailed commentary in footnotes, which here occupy up to 80 per cent of the page. There are copious references throughout, showing the breadth of Charles Bayne's reading on this subject. The article stimulated two comments in the 1908 volume of the *English Historical Review*: on pages 87-91 the Rev H. A. Wilson generally commends Bayne's analysis, but queries whether Elizabeth in fact withdrew; on pages 533-4 C. L. Ross offers a fuller text of what Il Schifanoya wrote.

Then Charles Bayne found some contrary evidence, which he felt bound to record. In the 1909 volume, on pages 322-3, he reports a Jesuit priest called Pedro de Ribadeneira, who was in London at the time, saying that the Spanish ambassador, de Feria, refused to attend the coronation because of irregularities in the mass. Though de Feria's own report did not survive, Charles Bayne was 'forced to revise my former opinion and to conclude that the significant rite of elevation was omitted'. The mass must have been celebrated by the Dean after all, not the Bishop, and Elizabeth did not withdraw.

Charles Bayne was rescued from this embarrassing position by Professor Albert Pollard, writing on pages 125-6 of the 1910 volume of the journal. Pollard first records a statement in 1570 by Elizabeth to the French ambassador that she had been crowned according the ceremonies of the catholic church, though she did not assist at the mass – i.e. she did withdraw after all. He then quotes the extant reply by Philip II to de Feria's lost despatch, which shows that the ambassador accompanied Elizabeth to the door of Westminster Abbey, but did not go in. De Feria withdrew because he *expected* the mass would not follow the full catholic rite, but in fact it did. So Charles Bayne's analysis was right all along.

Elizabeth's First Parliament

Despite its depth of learning, Charles Bayne's first article appears like a rehearsal for the dense research that underpins his second one, on 'Queen Elizabeth's First House of Commons', published in two parts in 1908. He sets out his objective clearly at the start of this second article. 'What was the composition of Queen Elizabeth's first parliament, which overthrew the Marian settlement of religion and finally severed the church of England from Rome? Was the official element exceptionally strong and did the government interfere with the elections more extensively than was usual?' He starts by examining the direct evidence used by several historians to claim that the House of Commons was packed with crown nominees. He finds that this evidence all dates from 1570 or later, while testimony from nearer the event is silent or admits of other interpretations. The most precise claim – that the government sent round lists of approved candidates – only dates from the 1630s and its context suggests special pleading. From this evidence he concludes 'the verdict must be one of non-proven' and then asks 'is a verdict of disproven possible?'

He now examines 'all the references to the elections that I have been able to discover in the records of the period.' He singles out six contests and shows that, while there was clearly interference by local magnates, like the earls of Bedford and Rutland, this was not done on the basis of a list of approved government candidates. In Surrey Lord Howard, who was very close to the crown, was unable to get his son accepted as a candidate. In Wiltshire the election was contested and Penruddock, the MP under Mary, soundly defeated Sir John Thynne of Longleat, an incomer linked to the government. Thynne conspired with Bronker, the local sheriff, to reverse this decision, but a later court ruling reinstated Penruddock and punished Bronker. Charles Bayne concludes that there were no government lists. He accepts that his sample is small, but it emerges from a much wider search in municipal archives. 'I have turned over as many of these volumes as I have been able to lay my hands on, yet I have found no trace of the story'.

This concludes the first part of the article. The second begins by asking: 'What was the actual composition of Elizabeth's first house of commons?' and seeks to discover any abnormal elements in it. From various sources Charles Bayne discovers the names of 356 of the 398 members. 25 per cent of these were 'old members', sitting in the same seat as they had under Mary, while 75 per cent were new. This looks like a major change, but he shows that in Mary's five parliaments the proportion of re-elected old members ranged from a high of 30 per cent to a low of 19 per cent. Thus, he concludes, 'The proportion of new members in Elizabeth's first parliament was not abnormally large'.

Charles Bayne then proceeds to a minute examination of the careers of the members, to discover which of them had held positions of trust under Mary. He examines the record of 130 holders of county seats in the parliaments of 1558 (under Mary) and 1559. Leading figures under Mary, such as her Privy Councillors, naturally disappear, to be replaced by their Elizabethan successors; but that does not constitute packing of the house. Out of 70 county members of Elizabeth's first parliament, 27 had been justices of the peace under Mary, who chose her JPs with care, and ten had been sheriffs. He next compares the 141 members known from two-seat boroughs, to see whether those elected in 1559 had local roots or were parachuted in. He finds a very high proportion of mayors, aldermen and other local figures in Elizabeth's parliament, almost as high as in Mary's time. He looks at the 121 members from smaller, single-seat boroughs, to see how many had links with court or government and finds only 21 per cent had such links. The only real evidence of government interference appears in the creation of new boroughs – but there were only three of these.

The article concludes that Elizabeth's first parliament 'stood high in the scale of independence among Tudor parliaments'.

The circulation of candidate lists was a fable. There was interference by local magnates, as always happened, but no systematic packing of the house by government. This was not surprising, as the election writs went out barely three weeks after Elizabeth's accession. 'The fragments that survive all point to the conclusion that there was little interference by the government.'

The Episcopal Visitation of 1559

After two solid articles in as many years, the third follows after a five year gap, which suggests that Charles Bayne wrote his book on Anglo-Roman relations first. But the third article, 'The Visitation of the Province of Canterbury, 1559', is closely linked to the other two, as the opening sentence shows: 'In this paper I deal with the proceedings of the commissioners who carried out the royal visitation of 1559 in the province of Canterbury and thereby took the first step towards bringing the 'alteration of religion' which was enacted by the parliament of 1559 into practical effect'. But unlike its two predecessors, which argued a case, this one aims to extract a coherent narrative from fragmentary evidence, supported by appendices of hitherto unpublished material.

Charles Bayne first establishes who were the visitors on the five circuits of the province, publishing a detailed list drawn up under the supervision of William Cecil, which survives in the Record Office. He then goes through the activities of each group, reconstructing their itinerary as far as possible. He pulls together evidence not only from official reports, memoirs, letters and pamphlets but also from records of court cases and from churchwardens' accounts. This analysis shows that everywhere the visitors required cathedral and parish clergy to accept Elizabeth as head of the church and the new services laid down by parliament. Those who resisted were removed, either at once or later, while those who had preached contrary doctrine were obliged to recant. Many parishes had incumbents restored who had been removed under Mary. Parishes also drew up inventories of church property and any 'Romish' items, like rood-lofts or marble altars, were destroyed.

The article ends with a discussion of when the visitation was wound up. It does not draw conclusions, but it attaches detailed appendices of court records, churchwardens' accounts and texts for recantations and the institution of vicars. Unlike all his other works, this article shows Charles Bayne as more interested in the process of extracting evidence from scattered and fragmentary data than in the conclusions that could be drawn from them. But this may suggest that in fact he found his sources less instructive than he had hoped. He may also have felt that after his concentration on Queen Elizabeth, he needed a new challenge and a different field of study. After 1913 he shifted his attention to King Henry VII.

Anglo-Roman Relations

The three articles analysed so far concentrate on what was happening in England in the first twelve months of Elizabeth's reign. Charles Bayne's book, *Anglo-Roman Relations, 1558-1565*, is more ambitious in scope. It deals with England's external relations, both directly with the Vatican and indirectly with the other powers of Europe – Spain, France, the Hapsburg empire and the protestant princes of Germany. It covers a rather longer time-span, though it is limited to Elizabeth's first six years, when first Paul IV and then Pius IV occupied the papal chair. It is based on a close reading of the diplomatic correspondence of the time. As Charles Bayne says in his preface:

'The materials used have been derived from original sources, principally the correspondence of the king of Spain with his ambassadors in Rome and the transcripts of Vatican manuscripts which are preserved at the Record Office. Unpublished state papers in the British Museum and a few more of which I procured copies from Paris, Vienna and Brussels, have furnished further information.'

Many of these documents make up the 68 appendices to the book. To read them, Charles Bayne needed to be fluent in five languages – English, French, Italian, Latin and Spanish; papal ambassadors wrote in Italian but imperial ones in Latin. But it does not appear that his researches took him out of England. Instead, he acknowledges help from those at the Spanish royal archives and elsewhere who copied the papers for him.

The book reveals the tensions between religious fervour and secular politics and the efforts of diplomacy to reconcile them. As such it is rich in paradoxes, which Charles Bayne delights in exposing. The irascible Pope Paul IV had fallen out with Queen Mary and her archbishop, Cardinal Pole, so that at first he welcomed Elizabeth's accession with relief. Elizabeth temporised so skilfully about her intentions for the church in England that Paul IV had taken no action against her before he died in August 1559.

The new pope, Pius IV, wanted to send an emissary to Elizabeth to discover her real intentions and, if necessary, to convey his displeasure. But his plans were upset by the rivalry between the kings of Spain and France, both of whom had hopes of acquiring the English throne: Philip II by marrying Elizabeth; François II through his wife, Mary Queen of Scots. So the first papal emissary was vetoed by Philip as being too confrontational, while the second was eventually refused entry to England by Cecil, as likely to provoke unrest. Philip soon married a princess of France and gave his backing to Robert Dudley, who promised he would restore the catholic faith if he married the queen. But such a marriage was intolerable to the English nobles, even the catholics among them, who 'preferred to sacrifice their religion rather than see the queen married to the least of them'.

Pius IV decided to reconvene the Council of Trent. This led to complex diplomatic manoeuvres to see whether the Council would meet under conditions that permitted delegations from England and the German protestant states to attend. The key player was France, where protestant influence was rising. But a complicated three-cornered exchange in Paris between Catherine de Medicis, the pope's envoy the Cardinal of Ferrara and the British ambassador to France eventually came to nothing. The Council began meeting on the pope's terms, with no protestants present.

However, despite the pressure from English catholics (including former bishops) in prison in London or exile in Flanders, the Council took no decisions against Elizabeth. The pope, full of zeal, endorsed a proposal that Elizabeth and her church should be excommunicated. But this was opposed by the emperor and the king of Spain, on the grounds that such a measure could not be enforced and would therefore bring the papacy and catholic Europe into disrepute in England. Pius IV backed off and the book ends with his death in December 1565.

The concluding chapter reviews the policies adopted by the three principal players – the Vatican, Spain and England. Pope Paul IV took no action against England. Pius IV vacillated between force and persuasion. All his attempts at force were headed off by Spain. But persuasion too was bound to fail, as neither side would compromise over papal authority. Philip II wanted a friendly England, despite religious difficulties, as Elizabeth held the balance between Spain and France. 'The conflicting sentiments by which he was influenced resulted in a singularly ineffective policy'. The consequence was 'to make him the best friend of the English reformation'. Elizabeth was not a committed reformer, like Cecil, and wanted a united, national church. But her Act of Supremacy (May 1559) 'made a declaration of war on the papacy'. Once Pius IV had recalled the Council of Trent, Elizabeth attempted to engage France, to avoid isolation, but France could not be tempted. 'In the end Elizabeth declined to take even the first step towards reconciliation with Rome'.

Charles Bayne's book as a whole illuminates the international movements of the time with great insight and clarity. It reveals his remarkable ability to expose and interpret the ambiguities and apparent contradictions of diplomatic exchanges, which have not changed much in the last 450 years. He also takes a strictly neutral position on religious issues, showing no partiality for Catholics, Anglicans, Lutherans or any other group. It was the last work that Charles Bayne published in his lifetime. He continued historical research leading to his final book, which appeared after his death. Yet he lived for over forty years after retiring from the ICS and it is necessary to look now at his personal and family life over that period.

Chapter 12

Family Life in Retirement

On return from Burma in 1906, Charles Bayne, like Peter Bayne before him, established himself and his family in the suburbs of London. But he did not lose touch with Burmese affairs. Soon after his return he was in contact with Sir Charles Crosthwaite, who had retired from the India Office Council and was beginning to gather material for his book *The Pacification of Burma*, which appeared in 1912. Crosthwaite wrote to Herbert White on 3 April 1907: 'Bayne is lunching with me in town tomorrow'. On 26 April he wrote: 'We hope (Mrs Nelson and I) to meet the Baynes in town next week', and on 3 May: 'Bayne and Mrs B met us in town on Wednesday and Mrs Nelson lunched us all at the Sesame Club'. But in fact Crosthwaite never made use of Charles Bayne when writing his book. He wrote again to White, on 13 April 1908: 'I have not had time to open up communications with Bayne' and on 20 August 1909: 'I have not seen Bayne or heard of him for a long time'.

The last reference to Bayne in Crosthwaite's correspondence is more significant. He wrote to Fanny, Lady White, on 15 October 1909: 'Bayne tells me his daughter is going out to you and Sir Herbert mentioned it. But [he] did not say when. I suppose she will be leaving soon'. This shows that Charles and Augusta remained close friends with Herbert and Fanny White, as they were preparing to send their eldest daughter Alice, aged 18, to stay at Government House for several months. While she was there, Alice, like her mother before her, met her future husband, Henry Stevenson. He was an ICS officer of 35, nearly twice her age, who had arrived in Burma in 1898 and was now serving at Yamethin in Upper Burma. Charles and Augusta would not have known him well, as his posts had all been outside Rangoon, while Alice herself had left Burma as a child before he got there. The couple were married at Maymyo on 27 April 1910, in what must have been a grand wedding laid on by the Whites less than a month before they left Burma. Both Herbert and Fanny White signed the register, as did Frank Gates, the Financial Commissioner, and the cantonment chaplain from Rangoon came up to take the service. Henry Stevenson served in Burma till 1933, rising to become Commissioner and being Chairman of the Rangoon Development Trust as his last post. The couple had no children.

From 1910 onwards, Charles Bayne acted as examiner in Burmese for the qualifying exam for the ICS. He approached this task in his usual conscientious way. More than 40 years later, some of those he examined could still remember him. Alan Gledhill (ICS Burma 1920-1948) wrote: 'He was a kind examiner, but he was not soft. He gave me a very long session, with the object of finding out what I did know, not what I didn't know. When later I had to examine others in Burmese, I followed very closely what he did on the occasion when I was examinee.' Henry Stevenson, his son-in-law, recorded Charles Bayne as telling him that he never been faced with the necessity of failing a candidate and could not have continued to hold the appointment if he had.

The main source for the family's life at this time is an album of photos from the years 1910-1911, taken by Madge with the camera she was given on her seventeenth birthday (22 November 1910), each photo carefully labelled and dated. The Baynes were then settled in Beckenham, next-door to Norwood, where Charles' father had lived at the end of his life. They occupied No 2 Oakwood Avenue, a substantial house on three floors with a large garden, and had probably moved there soon after Charles came back from Burma. Inside the house the photos show a spacious hall and staircase, a drawing-room with a piano and a large dining-room with bookcases. There was a study for Charles and a schoolroom, which suggest the girls were educated at home – Miss Rhys, who is often in the photos, may have been the governess. Each of the children had their own bedroom and there was at least one spare bedroom. There are many photos taken in the garden. A few show Charles gardening, wearing a boater hat. But most of the garden was a wide flat lawn, used for croquet (which Charles played in a bowler) and especially for tennis.

From the photos and some other sources it is possible to reconstruct the life of the different members of the family at the time. Charles appears in his study deeply engaged in his historical researches, with a massive volume on his knee and a desk piled with papers. But he also found time to relax with the newspaper and take tea in the garden. Augusta (who is revealed as slightly taller than Charles) is shown in kitchen, dining-room and garden, ready to strike poses for pictures. She had her own circle of friends – Mrs Cox, Mrs Simpson and a mysterious lady called 'Queen'. Alice does not appear in the album at all, as she was already in Burma as the wife of Henry Stevenson. One photo, dated 12 March 1911, shows 'Mr and Miss Stevenson', who may be his brother and sister.

Madge, the photographer, appears often – alone, with her brother Ronald or with various friends of her own age, often in tennis parties. One friend who features regularly was a young man called Budge Hall, the son of Charles's close Burma colleague William Hall. Madge went to Camberley to visit Budge and his parents, who were also in touch with Sir Charles Crosthwaite. (Crosthwaite told White on 10 October 1911: 'Hall and Mrs Hall came over from Camberley. He looks very fit and young. She has aged a good bit'.) Ronald, now aged 14, had decided that he wished to enter the Royal Navy. By this time he was attending Osborne College on the Isle of Wight.

Several pictures show him in his cadet's uniform, while in others he is bicycling or climbing trees.

Aunts and cousins are also featured in Madge's album. Aunt Clotilda, Charles' sister, visited Beckenham in December 1910. Her husband, the Rev Charles Marson, was now vicar of Hambridge, near Langport in Somerset. She would outlive her brother Charles, dying in 1952. Various members of the Dunlop family – Walter, Sybil and Colin, with their dog Rob – appear both at Beckenham and on holiday with the Baynes at Felixstowe ferry in August 1911. The Dunlops were cousins by marriage – Augusta's sister Esther May had married James Dunlop in Rangoon in 1889 – and Sybil later became a very successful silversmith. The family made some other excursions too. They went to the 'Festival of Empire' at the Crystal Palace on 12 September 1911 and visited Herne Bay for a week later in the month.

Charles Bayne made use of other members of his family to help him in his researches. In the preface to his book *Anglo-Roman Relations*, he expresses his gratitude 'to Miss Bayne and the Rev R. Bayne for help and advice on various points.' The Rev Ronald Bayne's involvement has already been noted, while Miss Bayne must be his youngest sister Jane Isabella, who never married and about whom very little is known. Both of them died in the early 1920s, with Isabella being buried with her stepmother Anna Mayo in Harlington churchyard. Later in the same preface Charles Bayne includes Fraulein Gerwien in the list of those who copied documents for him in Vienna and elsewhere. This shows that he was still in contact with members of his mother's family, nearly 50 years after her death.

After Madge's album, the family records become very sparse over the next twenty years and more. But it is clear that the First World War brought change and upheaval to the Bayne family, as to all households in Britain. In the course of the war the other children left home. Madge married a young army officer, David Aikenhead of the Royal Horse Artillery, in 1917 and they moved into his family home at Great Elm in Somerset. Ronald was commissioned in the Royal Navy in time to serve on a battleship, HMS Canada, in the battle of Jutland in 1916. Recruitment into the ICS dried up and so Charles Bayne was no longer required as examiner in Burmese after 1917, though he took it up again once the war ended. But the rapid inflation during the war eroded the value of his ICS pension and he took a temporary post at the Ministry of Pensions. This may have continued after the war, but he would have had to retire in 1925 on reaching the age of 65. With no children at home, Charles and Augusta left Oakwood Avenue and took a smaller house in Beckenham, at 14 Foxgrove Road, where they lived for the rest of their lives.

Even after the war ended, the Bayne children continued to be spread around the world. Alice and Henry were still in Burma. David Aikenhead's artillery regiment was posted to Iraq as part of the British occupying force. Madge gave birth to Robert, a first grandson for Charles and Augusta, in Basra in 1920. She soon brought him home, as he appears as a very small baby with Madge and Augusta in a photo taken in a Bromley studio. Augusta is stouter now and her hair is turning grey. A second Aikenhead grandchild, Jane, was born in 1923. The infant Jane was photographed in London with Madge and her grandfather who, at 63, looks a venerable gentleman with bald head and bushy white eyebrows and moustache (Plate VII.1). But he was still committed to his historical researches, as described in the next chapter.

Ronald ended the war as a lieutenant RN. He spent the 1920s partly in training as a gunnery officer and partly with the South China fleet, ending the decade as a lieutenant commander. In 1931 he married Elizabeth (Betty) Bayne, my mother. The wedding photos show Charles Bayne looking aged alongside the bride's parents, who were twenty years younger, but he still appears fit and active for his 70 years. Augusta, however, could not be at the wedding. She was now suffering from heart disease and her angina made her a semi-invalid.

Ronald's marriage produced two more grandchildren; Christopher in 1933 and Nicholas in 1937. The last surviving photo of Charles and Augusta (Plate VII.2) shows them in the garden at Foxgrove Road, admiring Christopher aged about three months. Ronald's naval postings in the 1930s included Malta and a return to China, with promotion to commander. He was second-in-command of the battleship HMS Resolution, based at Plymouth, as the Second World War approached.

In the last decade of Charles Bayne's life some personal correspondence at last becomes available. The longest sequence of letters relate to his last book on Henry VII and are covered in the next chapter, but they include some asides about his private life at the time. He is happy to come up to London in October 1938 to meet Professor Plucknett of the Selden Society, but prefers to do so in the hours of daylight and adds: 'Don't expect me if there is a fog. I am too old to come to London in a fog.' By May 1939 he is employing a copyist, as his eyes can no longer make out the original Tudor manuscripts. But he is still going up to the Record Office, while his handwriting is as clear, firm and elegant as ever.

At the same time, he is able to engage in some genealogical research on Augusta's family. Charles Newbold, a partner in Hodgkinson and Beevor, the solicitors founded by her grandfather, writes several letters during 1939 with queries about the people named in papers held by the firm. Charles Bayne's notes and draft replies are preserved in the Hodgkinson papers and contain information about the family that has already been used in Chapter 5. The correspondence also includes items from Charles and Augusta's life before they met and reminiscences about their ICS days. Charles notes that Augusta's uncle, the Rev Robert Hodgkinson, was the senior mathematics master at Uppingham School when he was there in the 1870s. When Colonel Walter Beevor, a cousin of Augusta's through her grandmother, is found dead in a London cab, Charles Bayne writes on 19 November 1939: 'Isn't it odd that that letter about Walter Beevor should appear in yesterday's *Times*. My wife knew him well when she was a girl, and we met him at the Delhi Durbar of 1903 when he was on the staff of the Duke of Connaught.'

A few letters survive from Charles and Augusta to their son Ronald and his wife Betty during the early years of the Second World War. Charles writes to Ronald in Plymouth on 7 September 1939: 'I don't suppose the outbreak of war made much difference to you, as you can't be busier'. From his garden he had a fine view of barrage balloons and had become accustomed to air raid alarms at 2.30 and 7 am. 'When they occur, your mother, I and the two servants come down to the drawing room, shut the shutters and sit at the back of the room under your Nelson portrait till the all-clear sounds.' No 14 Foxgrove Road came through the war untouched, though flying bombs fell nearby in 1944. The Nelson portrait now hangs on my brother Christopher's walls.

On 29 January 1940, Charles and Augusta marked their golden wedding, thanking Madge and Ronald for the telegrams they sent. But they did not put an announcement in *The Times*, 'because we think celebrations are out of place when we are at war'. A year later they were expressing their sympathy with Ronald and Betty, still stationed at Plymouth, for having to send their children away to Yorkshire. On 10 February Augusta writes to Betty: 'I suppose the raids got so bad with you so you thought it wiser to send them away from them. When will this cursed war end? I hope Christopher will like his school. I will print him a letter before long and we have not forgotten that Nicholas' birthday is on Saturday.'

This was Augusta's last letter. She had long suffered from heart disease and died suddenly on 22 February 1941, the day before her 77th birthday. That left Charles, in his 80s, alone in Beckenham with his faithful cook Mary Ann Nash, to whom he left £100 in his will. But fortunately Ronald was soon to be appointed to a position in the Admiralty, with the rank of captain. This enabled Ronald to settle his family in Oxford (where Charles Bayne's youngest grandchild David was born in 1944) and see them at weekends, while he stayed with his father during the working week. My brothers and I used to be taken to visit him from Oxford for the day occasionally and we were also all together at Great Elm, where Aunt Madge presided, for Christmas in 1945. I only remember him dimly, as a frail old gentleman with a large moustache who lived off soup and rice pudding. But Charles Bayne was still working on his book about the Council of Henry VII and continued right up to his death. The story of that belongs in the next chapter.

Chapter 13

Late Research: King Henry VII

After three solid articles and a book on Queen Elizabeth's religious policies, Charles Bayne decided to change both the period and the underlying theme of his research. He moved from the last Tudor monarch to the first and changed from the politics of religion to the administration of justice. He chose to study the role of the Council of King Henry VII as a court of law and to write another book on it. It is not clear why he made this change, but there are some clues. Once again Charles' brother Ronald was probably influential, not only because of his own interest in the early Tudors but also by introducing Charles to Professor Albert Pollard. The Rev Ronald Bayne would have known Pollard through the *DNB*, where he was assistant editor from 1893 to 1903, when he was appointed Professor of Constitutional History at University College London. As Chapter 11 showed, Pollard rescued Charles Bayne from an awkward dilemma over the coronation of Elizabeth I.

Over the next 30 years Professor Pollard became a leading figure in historical studies, being the founder of the Institute of Historical Research. He was the greatest authority on the Tudor period of his day, concentrating mainly on Henry VIII. But his works include *The Reign of Henry VII from Contemporary Sources*, published in 1914, and three solid articles in the *English Historical Review* for 1922-23 on the Council, Star Chamber and Privy Council under the Tudors. From later correspondence it is clear that he admired Charles Bayne's work, so he may well have suggested to him that the legal role of Henry VII's Council, including the Court of Star Chamber, deserved closer study. Charles Bayne was already familiar with the Court of Star Chamber under Elizabeth and had used its cases as sources for his earlier articles. So he was ready to engage in this new field.

As long as Charles Bayne had a full-time job at the Ministry of Pensions, he could not devote himself fully to research. But from 1925, and possibly earlier, Charles Bayne began working through all the available records of the Council of Henry VII, as preserved in the state papers in the Record Office and elsewhere. He brought together his findings in a monograph that, in about 150,000 words, explained the general role and composition of the Council and then focused on its two legal aspects, as Court of Star Chamber and Court of Requests. The manuscript of his book called *The Council of Henry VII* was complete by the end of 1934. Though it was not published till much later, this is the best opportunity to summarise its contents.

The Council of Henry VII

The traditional view of the Star Chamber is that it was a principal instrument by which Henry VII established order in his kingdom. Charles Bayne goes back to the original sources to create a very different picture. The main sources for the operation of Henry's Council are entries from its daily registers. These, however, exist only in later copies of selected extracts, mainly in the *Liber Intrationum*. The judicial work of the Star Chamber is known from records of pleadings, though these have suffered from later neglect and are often incomplete. There are fuller records of the Court of Requests, which tried minor civil cases, but this part of Charles Bayne's monograph – about 30 per cent – was never published and does not survive.

The Council under Henry VII was very different from the Privy Council that emerged under the later Tudors. Its membership was much larger, with a strong presence from the church (the experts in canon and civil law) and from the legal profession. This was because the Council made no distinction between its executive and its judicial role. Like his medieval predecessors, Henry VII believed the monarch should be accessible to his subjects, though 'his functions as judge came to devolve largely on his Council'. Within a large total membership, there was a small group of officials who were nearly always present, either ex officio, like the Lord Chancellor, Lord Treasurer and Lord Privy Seal, or because of personal links to Henry. They formed an 'inner ring of habitual advisers', the fore-runner of the later Privy Council. Diplomatic correspondence showed the king consulting the Council on foreign policy, both in formal sessions and in small informal groups, but Henry 'always had the last word'. The Council was rarely visible in domestic measures, but Charles Bayne concludes: 'It was an essential part of the machinery of government.'

The judicial aspect of the Council is habitually known as the Court of Star Chamber. But this title only became common under Henry VIII, when the court tried major criminal cases brought by the Crown. An Act of 1487, with the title 'Pro Camera Stellata, an Acte giving the Court of Starchamber authority to punish divers misdemeanours', had long been regarded as the origin of the court. But Charles Bayne shows that the title had been added later to the parliament roll recording the act, which in fact created a court that differed 'in personnel, jurisdiction and powers' from what became the Star Chamber. In Charles Bayne's view, the court created by the act of 1487 was one of several experimental special tribunals which did not survive Henry VII's reign, as the Council found it did not need these extra powers. Under Henry VII, 'Star Chamber' meant the place in Westminster where members of the Council sat as a court to try both criminal and civil cases, almost all brought by private persons.

Litigation in the Star Chamber began when the plaintiff approached the court 'as able to right wrongs of every kind. It could be appealed to for help when other remedies had failed or were unavailable.' The defendant would be summoned to appear and was bound by an oath. Then the court could examine defendant, plaintiff and witnesses, using a very fluid procedure. In one important case, where Damsel sought redress against a false accusation of theft by Green, the court conducted four separate examinations of Green. The Star Chamber was thus 'meting out justice to criminals beyond the reach of common law'. It also acted promptly, in contrast to the common law, which was notoriously dilatory.

By far the most common charge tried by the court was rioting, which provided 115 out of 194 extant cases. These cases were not brought by the Crown, which preferred to use the courts of common law against rioters, but by private persons. About three-quarters of them were really disputes about land. Claimants forcibly removed from their property would bring a case of riot in order to get the attention of the Star Chamber. The remaining quarter contained picturesque details of actual riots and 'serious disturbances of the peace', but on closer inspection they turned out to be very mild, with few injuries and no deaths.

Other criminal cases reaching the Star Chamber showed 'no ingenious or unusual evil-doing', but were all commonplace offences. Their one common feature was that they 'could not have been pursued under common law'. There were 43 known civil suits, half again being land disputes. Two of these showed the Star Chamber protecting citizens against powerful local magnates; otherwise it was hard to see why it was involved at all. Finally eleven cases dealt with administrative disputes involving monasteries, civic authorities and trading bodies. Here the common law had no machinery and the Star Chamber provided the supreme authority needed, though it did not always enforce its decisions.

Finally, Charles Bayne notes that Henry VII often enforced physical punishment or heavy summary fines on his own authority. In contrast, the Star Chamber imposed only light penalties, limited to fines or short spells in jail till fines should be paid. 'The most striking characteristic of the Court was its moderation. It was surely the mildest-mannered tribunal that ever sentenced a criminal, failing altogether to live up to the reputation of ruthlessness that the Star Chamber has enjoyed since the seventeenth century.'

Finding a Publisher

Having finished his book, Charles Bayne began to look for a publisher. The story of his quest is told in the largest surviving collection of his personal letters, exchanged with academic contacts. His earliest letter, dated 16 August 1937, sets the scene:

'The history of my book *The Council of King Henry VII* is short. I finished it at the end of 1934 and sent it to the Clarendon Press, which published a book of mine in 1913 (*Anglo-Roman Relations, 1558-1565*). They sent it back in less than three weeks with a polite letter saying that they could not afford to publish as many learned and unremunerative works as they could wish. A year later I sent it to the Cambridge University Press at the suggestion of Professor Pollard, who had read the MS in the interval and thought highly of it. I was extremely gratified by his good opinion and most grateful to him for the trouble he took over the book. The Cambridge Press kept it for several months and, I have no doubt, gave it full consideration. But their verdict was the same as that of the Clarendon Press, namely, that in view of many other unremunerative commitments they regretted their inability to publish it. Last month I sent the MS to Jonathan Cape at the suggestion of Professor H Bellot. The result you know.'

Jonathan Cape's reader had decided the work was too technical to be published by a commercial publisher without a subsidy.

But Charles Bayne's luck was about to change. Mr Jonathan Cape himself sent the book to Professor John Neale, who had taken over Pollard's chair at University College London. Neale, whose main academic work was on Queen Elizabeth I, knew Charles Bayne's earlier work and had already heard of the book's existence. He was so impressed by its quality that he was determined to get it published. As he wrote to Charles Bayne: 'I should think myself a poor worm if I didn't offer to do anything that it is in my power to do in order to secure its publication.' With Charles Bayne's active encouragement, Neale first submitted it to Manchester University Press, where he had been professor, but this got nowhere. Then, following another suggestion from Professor Hugh Bellot, he approached Professor Theodore Plucknett, Professor of Legal History at the London School of Economics. This proved a decisive move. Plucknett had just become one of the three literary directors of the Selden Society, a learned society dedicated to the historical study of English law. While the Society did not publish monographs, it did publish collections of legal texts. Plucknett agreed to see if the Selden Society could publish Charles Bayne's book as the introduction to a collection or collections of cases brought before the Council of Henry VII.

Professor Plucknett warned Neale, in a letter of 2 December 1937, 'The society moves very slowly'. The negotiations over the book occupied the whole of the next twelve months. First Plucknett read the manuscript. It would have appealed to his love of extracting historical testimony from difficult sources and it came with a strong letter of support from Professor Pollard. Plucknett gave a positive recommendation to his fellow directors in the Society and on 17 June 1938 he wrote to Charles Bayne to report their provisional decision. 'The Society has so far published only collections of original documents, but many of our volumes contain introductions which are in effect substantial monographs on the same scale as your own.' He invited Charles Bayne to assemble up to three volumes of 'select cases' from the Council of Henry VII, dividing his monograph between the different collections. He added that the Society would pay an editorial fee to cover the expenses of transcribing the documents to be published.

Charles Bayne replied on 19 June: 'I should naturally prefer to see my book published as it stands but I should nevertheless be gratified if the scheme you suggest were adopted.' He accepted the fee provided it covered, but did not exceed, the transcription costs. 'For private reasons I don't feel justified in spending money on my hobby, but on the other hand I should not like to think that a learned society was paying me for what I much prefer to do for nothing.' Stuart Moore, the Secretary of the Society, then wrote in July to confirm the proposal and suggest meetings 'after the Long Vacation'. In October 1938 Charles Bayne had meetings with Moore and Plucknett and agreed on the scope of his work and the conditions for producing it.

The original suggestion had been for three volumes – one on the Council generally, one on the Star Chamber and one on the Court of Requests. But it soon appeared that there were not enough documents to include in the first of these, so the agreement was to produce two volumes, the former taking Council and Star Chamber together and the latter the Court of Requests, each with its own introduction. Charles Bayne was already beginning to identify the cases and other documents to be included in the first volume and the list of cases he produced at this stage matches closely what was finally published. Throughout the negotiations Charles Bayne insisted that the introductions should incorporate his monograph in full, which should not be shortened to make room for more documents. 'Not that I would mind seeing my work cut about', he wrote, 'but I doubt whether I am equal to the labour involved. It would mean re-writing my book. The book could not be reduced in size by cutting out chunks here and there.'

By the beginning of 1939, as Charles Bayne began his 79th year, the negotiations were complete. On 16 January Moore, the Secretary, wrote to Charles Bayne: 'The Council of the Selden Society at its meeting in December authorised me to enter into agreements with you to edit volumes for the Society.' He enclosed an agreement which Charles Bayne signed at once, undertaking 'to edit for the Selden Society two volumes of Documents and Select Cases in the Council of Henry VII'. Only then did Charles Bayne feel confident enough to write to Professors Neale, Pollard and Bellot to report this happy outcome and to thank them for all their efforts on his behalf – the letters are worth quoting.   To Pollard he wrote: 'I feel it is to you, in the first place, that I owe this, to me, gratifying result. But for your kind efforts in 1935 and 1936 my book would certainly be still reposing in the cupboard to which I consigned it when the Clarendon Press turned it down.' To Bellot: 'Every time my poor book got stuck in a rut, your powerful efforts levered it out.' To Neale: 'I am aware how much I am indebted to you for all you have done to bring my poor book safely to port.' All the professors wrote back to say how delighted they were at this result, with Pollard adding: 'I congratulate you on the satisfaction of your hope deferred.

   Charles Bayne had written to Professor Pollard: 'I daresay there will be some delay before it appears in print, but barring accidents it should appear sooner or later.' At first the work moved ahead rapidly. In January 1939 the Huntington Library in California agreed to provide copies of their manuscript (from the Bridgewater Collection) of the *Liber Intrationum*, the key source for the acts of Henry VII's Council. In May Charles Bayne was writing enthusiastically to Plucknett: 'I am afraid I have been outrunning the constable in collecting matter for the first volume.' Both the material from California and the selected Star Chamber cases were longer than he had thought:

'It is ten years or more since I read the originals [of the cases] and my memory of them had become dim. I may add that I find them extremely interesting and my copyist, who has read a lot of medieval literature, is very impressed with them. The value of my collection would be much impaired if I had to eliminate any of the material already collected and there are several more cases of great interest that I would like to add.'

Plucknett, after consulting the Secretary, was reassuring: 'You need not consider yourself bound by the number of sheets in your contract. So do not stint us of anything which you judge to be of value.'

At this point there is an eight-year gap in the letters. But it is clear that the outbreak of the Second World War created many obstacles. As Professor Plucknett reported in his Preface to the published volume:

> 'The long and arduous process of securing rotographs and transcripts and then of setting up the mass of material upon which the massive monograph had been based occupied the next few years, although printing and publishing conditions immediately after the war were not easy. At the same time, the author had also in mind a project of dealing with the Court of Requests. This project had to be abandoned.'

However, the correspondence resumes with a letter of 17 September 1947 to Charles Bayne from Spottiswoode and Ballantyne, the printers who were now setting up the proofs of the book. In response to their queries Charles Bayne replied on 19 September, in a shaky but legible hand: 'I return the slips of proof you sent me and have noted on the margin the style which I prefer. Will you kindly print accordingly throughout? I am ready for more proof whenever you send it.' This is the last surviving letter from Charles Bayne. On 6 December 1947 he died, two days after his 87th birthday.

Posthumous Publication and Final Tributes

Professor Plucknett and Stuart Moore were still at the Selden Society and were not going to abandon Charles Bayne's work, having got so far. Much of the text of the documents, though not all, had been set up in proof form, while the introduction existed in a complete typescript. After some delay the Selden Society purchased the copyright of the volume from Charles Bayne's executors (his children Ronald and Alice) and persuaded Professor C. H Williams, Professor of History at King's College London, to take on the final editing necessary.

Unfortunately Professor Williams had too many other responsibilities and sat on the book for several years without doing anything. The Selden Society, whose Secretary was now Howard Drake, finally took it away from him in 1955 and gave it to Professor William Dunham of Yale University. Dunham had edited an earlier volume for the Society and also worked on the Huntington manuscripts of the *Liber Intrationum*.

Professor Dunham moved with speed, so that by the end of the year Howard Drake could report to Ronald:

> 'All the text [of the documents] is now set in page proof and has been passed for press. Your father's long and interesting introduction has been set up in galley proof and after revision has been reset in page proof. There remains an index to prepare and Professor Dunham is planning to add a short postscript to the introduction commenting on your father's views about the Council.'

The index took more time, but was eventually prepared by Marian Dale of the Institute of Historical Research, who also tidied up some loose ends left by Professor Dunham. The book was finally published as volume 75 in the publications of the Selden Society for 1956, though it actually appeared in 1958. It includes a photograph of Charles Bayne looking suitably scholarly (Plate VIII).

The volume is called: '*Select Cases in the Council of Henry VII*, edited for the Selden society by the late C. G. Bayne, CSI, and completed by William Huse Dunham, Jr.' But Professor Dunham never produced his postscript. There is no evidence that either he or Professor Williams added anything except one or two footnotes early in the book. Not only the introduction but all the preparation and editing of the texts should be regarded as the work of Charles Bayne. The texts occupy just over half of the printed volume and are nearly all summarised in the introduction based on his monograph. Where necessary, Charles Bayne has provided English translations alongside the original Latin texts and suggested missing words where the manuscripts are torn or otherwise illegible. He has annotated the texts fully, identifying people and places, explaining obscure and archaic words like 'barraters' (hired bullies) and 'nyghtertale' (night) and giving cross-references to other cases.

In this published version, however, there is some suspicion that Charles Bayne's monograph has been cut down, despite his earlier instructions. The introduction is slightly shorter than the original correspondence would suggest. It begins abruptly, with no statement of the aim of the work, and tails off without drawing together its conclusions. It does not recognise – as Charles Bayne would surely have done – the earlier work of I. S. Leadam, who had published a collection of Henry VII's Star Chamber cases for the Selden Society in 1903. It could be that Professor Plucknett, or Professor Dunham under his instructions, trimmed Charles Bayne's monograph so as to give more prominence to the new publication of legal texts. As a result this is perhaps the least accessible of Charles Bayne's historical writings, which only gives up its findings to the attentive reader of the whole.

The posthumous publication of this volume provided a final link with Burma. Professor Plucknett, though now often ill, prepared a memoir of Charles Bayne to serve as preface. Most of this dealt with the genesis of the volume and with Charles Bayne's earlier scholarly publications. But Plucknett wanted to include a passage about his ICS career in Burma. So Howard Drake sought the help of Alan Gledhill, Professor of Oriental Laws at the School of Oriental Studies, who had been a judge in Burma. Gledhill tried to contact former ICS officers who had served with Charles Bayne in Burma and still remembered him. But the results were scanty, as it was now over 50 years since he had left Burma. Those few ICS officers that survived from that period were too junior to have known him well, though several, including Gledhill himself, recalled him as the ICS examiner in Burmese.

Two eloquent tributes, however, came from Charles Dunn, who joined in 1900, and his son-in-law Henry Stevenson, who arrived in 1898. Charles Dunn recorded: 'I remember him as an august but benevolent Chief Secretary, whose handwriting, incidentally, was faultless. There were men of good abilities then but he excelled as a Secretary in an ICS Government. He was worthy of being better remembered by his juniors.' Henry Stevenson, after listing his academic publications, wrote: 'In all these works he showed the good judgement, deep scholarship, meticulous study and lucidity of style that had won him distinction in his service in Burma.' These comments lead naturally into the assessment of Charles Bayne as administrator and historian, set out in the next and final chapter.

Chapter 14

Charles Bayne as Administrator and Historian

This memoir is about the life and work of Charles Bayne. The sources for his life, especially his private life, are very fragmentary, so that the preceding chapters may contain many errors and misjudgements. But his work as a colonial administrator in Burma and as a Tudor historian is well documented, through the India Office records and through his own books and articles. So this final chapter seeks to assess his achievements in these two fields, looking back from a century after his retirement from the Indian Civil Service and fifty years after his last historical work was published.

Burmese Administrator

Charles Bayne had a very unusual career in the ICS. He was never in charge of a district, but spent 80 per cent of his time in Rangoon as part of the central administration. Although the Secretariat was often satirised for bureaucracy and red tape, in fact it attracted the more gifted ICS officers and Charles Bayne earned the confidence of successive Chief Commissioners and Lieutenant Governors. His time in the Secretariat covered a period when the central administration in Burma was under intense pressure, as Lord Curzon grudgingly recognised. Responsibilities were shifting away from the officers in the field to be concentrated in Rangoon. But the Secretariat was very thinly staffed and the development of a complete bureaucratic apparatus only began in Charles Bayne's final years.

Yet Charles Bayne and his colleagues did not enjoy great influence over colonial policy in Burma. The centralising trend meant that policy was made in Calcutta and largely ignored the distinctive qualities of Burma, a late addition to the Indian Empire. The provincial government had to follow instructions, with only limited discretion. Before Herbert White all the heads of the provincial government had made their careers in India before coming to Burma and this conditioned their attitude. Those who, like Charles Bernard, were sensitive to local conditions had little success in getting Calcutta to listen to them. But a strong-minded man like Charles Crosthwaite could impose policies which made sense in India, without reflecting on whether they would work in Burma as he intended.

'The period 1890-1920 could be termed the Golden Period of British rule', wrote the Burmese historian Htin Aung in 1965:

'The Burmese by 1890 had ceased to feel bitter against the British, firstly because the British re-introduced order and discipline in the country and secondly because, contrary to expectation, British rule did not affect the general structure of their society. The Burmese were fortunate that during the period 1890-1920, they were ruled by British officials who treated then with tact and sympathy. After the pacification of the country, Burmese nationalism became dormant until about 1910.'

In today's perspective, however, after forty years of Burmese isolation and in the shadow of the US occupation of Iraq, this judgement may be too charitable. It is necessary to consider whether Britain's colonial rule in my grandfather's time, even if benevolent in intention, lay at the root of Burma's later troubles. There are two reasons to think so, one political and one economic.

Like the Americans in Iraq in 2003, the British destroyed the Kingdom of Burma without having considered the consequences. The monarchy had provided a focus of national identity, even for Burmese living under British rule. Annexation to the British Empire and amalgamation with India destroyed this source of national identity and cohesion, without putting anything in its place. The Buddhist church, which was linked to the monarchy and provided another source of cohesion, was given no encouragement. The colonial administration, with its hierarchy spreading out from the Lieutenant Governor, was orderly and efficient and welcomed for that reason. But it was only an administration, not a government or political system like the monarchy it replaced. At the level of national government, the colonial period created a vacuum.

Of course, most Burmese had given little thought to the king in Mandalay and were more concerned with their local society. But the reforms in village administration, introduced by Crosthwaite on the basis of his experience in India, removed the foundations even of that. Crosthwaite asserted: 'It was known there was generally a headman to each village', whose primitive powers had been superseded by other local officials in 'a somewhat complicated hierarchy'. But there were no grounds for this assertion, which ignored the traditional respect shown by Burmese communities to their *myothugyis*. Crosthwaite's reforms were only introduced gradually, as existing *thugyis* died out, and their full consequences did not appear till after Charles Bayne had left Burma. But inexorably they undermined the centres of authority that Burmese recognised as their own and replaced them by structures imposed from outside.

Thus the systems introduced by the British never took root in Burma, either at the national level or among local communities. As a result, when political movements began to gather strength, even with British encouragement, they inevitably started from opposition to the colonial administration. Neither the monarchy nor the colonial administration had given the Burmese the foundations on which to construct a national government with democratic legitimacy.

The political upheavals from the 1920s onwards and the wartime occupation by Japan cut Burma loose from the institutions inspired by Britain without putting anything in their place. This has led to the isolationist despotism that has prevailed in Burma since the 1960s and resisted all efforts to overthrow it.

These political legacies were aggravated by economic ones. As Htin Aung records: 'The economic structure of Burmese society collapsed under the impact of the British conquest'. The Burmese economy had traditionally been inward-looking, based on self-sufficient agriculture. External trade had been a royal monopoly. But from the last quarter of the 19th century Burma became exposed to forces of economic globalisation as pervasive as those familiar to us a century later. The country had great potential wealth, especially from rapidly increasing rice production and carefully managed forest resources. But the native population was quite unprepared for this wealth and the obligations it brought along with its advantages. The Burmese rice farmers were squeezed between the big British purchasing firms and the Indian and native money-lenders. From being moderately prosperous farmers, secure on their land, they went to being struggling tenants or labourers with no property rights at all. The colonial government's attempts to correct this trend came to nothing.

There was no barrier to migration into British Burma from other parts of India. As the Burmese economy diversified with growing wealth, it was often Indian, Chinese and other immigrants that gained the benefit, not the local inhabitants. This happened with Indian Chettyar money-lenders in agriculture, but was even more serious in industry and services. As manufacturing developed and Rangoon became the third largest port of India, the docks and factories mainly employed Indian migrant workers. In the public service, Indians made up a large part of the police and often took civil servant posts that did not depend on local knowledge. For their part, the Chinese dominated internal trade and the construction industry. British and other European expatriates controlled timber and oil exploitation and the export business. By the early 1900s Burmese made up only one-third of the population of Rangoon, by far the richest and most modern city. The upshot was that the Burmese saw their traditional attachment to the land being undermined, while the new wealth of the country was going to foreigners, especially British expatriates or Indians. This created deep feelings of resentment and a reversion to the inward-looking economic instincts of the Burmese monarchy, which persist to this day.

Charles Bayne must take his share of responsibility for these political and economic failures. But the record suggests that he realised what was going wrong and did what he could to improve matters. As Secretary under Crosthwaite he was involved in justifying the harsh policy of pacification and preparing the reforms of local administration that later caused such damage. From his close association with his future brother-in-law George Hodgkinson and his fellow Scot Donald Smeaton, he would have understood the merits of a more conciliatory approach to the Burmese, which built on their local practices and traditions. But in his fairly junior position he could do little to influence his determined chief, who was convinced that Burma's problems could only be solved through measures that worked elsewhere in India.

As Revenue Secretary under Fryer, Charles Bayne tried to protect the Burmese forests from the abusive practices of the Bombay-Burma Trading Corporation, who showed all the predatory qualities attributed to multinational companies today. His most ambitious plan, to bring all the forests under government control, did not succeed, though he dared to advocate it to the Viceroy in person. But he and his colleagues did succeed in laying down an effective legal and contractual regime for managing the forests, which served Burma well far into the 20th century.

Charles Bayne shared the analysis, worked out by Donald Smeaton as Financial Commissioner, of the evils threatening the Burmese rice farmers. He perceived that the farmers were steadily being driven off the land and replaced by absentee landlords, at a time when many of his colleagues, including his chief Sir Frederic Fryer, denied the problem was urgent. But the solutions favoured by Smeaton were too puritanical in spirit to gain acceptance, while his confrontational manner turned everyone against him. When Charles Bayne himself came to officiate as Financial Commissioner, he maintained the pressure for legislation to protect the rice farmers. But he looked for solutions that made economic sense, as far as possible, and would limit the burdens imposed on the administration. His ideas were largely adopted by Herbert White, though they failed to overcome the resistance from vested interests in Burma. These efforts at reform were not helped by the attitude taken by Calcutta, which would criticise the Burmese government for inaction, but then reject or ignore any proposals they might make.

Even if they had been adopted, Charles Bayne's ideas for checking land alienation might well not have worked. As long as the farmers wanted money to finance their operations, the money-lenders would have found ways round the regulations and absentee landlords would have increased. Probably the only long-term solution would have been for the provincial government itself to provide finance for the farmers, on terms which drove the other money-lenders out of business. The government did make modest efforts to do this, but they were under-resourced and Calcutta would have been reluctant to fund anything more ambitious. But at least Charles Bayne, Donald Smeaton and Herbert White recognised the gravity of the problem and tried to correct it. Once White retired, the Burmese government went back into a state of denial, even though conditions for the farmers grew much worse. No serious action was taken until Burma was detached from India in 1935.

Charles Bayne was a hard-working, dedicated civil servant, with a strong sense of duty inherited, through his father, from his Scottish ancestors. He sustained a tremendous burden of work in an unhealthy climate over a very long period. This brought him twice to the point of breakdown, though, unlike Edward Symes, both times he was able to recover. He was constrained by his loyalty to his superiors, even when he disagreed with them over politics, as with Crosthwaite, or economics, as with Fryer. He interpreted his duty as being to carry out the instructions of his chief, even to the point of putting his signature to statements he knew were wrong or ill-judged.

Thus he was never an outspoken critic of government like Smeaton, who was prepared to defy his instructions. But he could see that mistakes had been made that were not being redressed. He may well have realised that he had left Burma at the peak of the British administration and the picture would soon begin to darken. He might not have foreseen the troubles ahead for Burma, but he would have understood why they happened. By the time he died, just a month before Burma became independent, he would have been saddened by the travails of the country he had helped to govern. What has happened since would have distressed him even more.

Tudor Historian

Yet right from the beginning of his retirement, Burma took second place in Charles Bayne's life. Research into Tudor history became his dominant activity. His published works represent only the visible part of a huge iceberg of meticulous research. His articles and books are far removed from popular history and make no concessions to the reader. He writes with impeccable clarity and even his most complex and subtle arguments are easy to follow. But he is clearly writing for other historians, not for the general public. He does not choose grand themes, but rather neglected aspects of history, where he can provide new insights and challenge the conventional wisdom. How far he succeeded in doing this can best be judged from his links with three leading Tudor historians of the 20th century: Albert Pollard, Sir John Neale and Sir Geoffrey Elton.

Charles Bayne knew Professor Pollard, as we have seen, and probably regarded him as his mentor. He was indebted to Pollard for his intervention over Elizabeth's coronation and may have moved over to study Henry VII at his prompting. Most of Pollard's work was on the early Tudors and his books on *Henry VIII* (1902) and *Cardinal Wolsey* (1929) are considered his masterpieces. But in 1919 he published *The History of England from the Accession of Edward VI to the Death of Elizabeth (1547-1603)*, volume 6 of 'The Political History of England' edited by Hunt and Poole. Pages 199-200, which deal with Queen Elizabeth's accession, draw heavily on Charles Bayne's articles on her coronation and her first House of Commons, reproducing their arguments. Pollard cites both articles, as well as his own coronation note, while on page 217 he has an indirect reference to Bayne's article on the 1559 Visitation – the only reference to this work that I have found.

For his part Charles Bayne, in his book on Henry VII's Council, draws on the articles by Pollard in the *English Historical Review* for 1922-23, which queried the link between the Star Chamber and the Act of 1487 believed to have created it. Bayne was not in awe of his mentor and was quite ready to assert that some of Pollard's views were 'not substantiated by the facts'. (He was equally ready, in the same volume, to dismiss theories advanced by his patron Professor Plucknett.) Pollard, as already noted, was sufficiently impressed by the book to recommend it first to the Cambridge University Press and then to the Selden Society, though he was already retired.

Professor John Neale succeeded to the chair of history at University College London after Pollard's retirement in 1931 and, as recorded in the last chapter, he was instrumental in getting Charles Bayne's last book published. As the DNB puts it, 'that Neale became the historian of Elizabethan England (of his generation) was doubtless a consequence of Pollard's reluctance to share Henry VIII with anyone else'. His most scholarly work was on Elizabeth's parliaments: *The Elizabethan House of Commons* in 1949 and *Elizabeth and Her Parliaments* in two volumes in 1953. Neale draws extensively on Charles Bayne's research in the passage dealing with the 1559 election in the first volume of *Elizabeth and Her Parliaments* (pages 38-40) and cites his article. The passage concludes: 'The old legend which made this a packed parliament was not only needless: it was bad psychology. Having long ago been demolished factually, it should be regarded as doubly defunct'.

Later in his life (he died in 1975) Sir John Neale became a strong advocate of what he called 'the biographical approach to history' and stimulated research into the lives of all those who sat in Elizabeth's parliaments. In doing this, he claimed to be following the pattern of Sir Lewis Namier's work on the parliaments of the 18th century. But in fact Charles Bayne's 1908 article was a much earlier example of this biographical approach, since his conclusions depended on exhaustive research into the origins and careers of the members of the parliaments of 1558 and 1559. However, Neale's reputation in Elizabethan parliamentary studies became so strong that he always tended to be cited as the authority and Charles Bayne's work in this area dropped out of sight.

Charles Bayne's book *Anglo-Roman Relations 1558-1565* made less impact than his parliamentary research and I have not been able to track down a review of it. It is listed with three other books as being 'indispensable' in the bibliography to J. B. Black's *The Reign of Elizabeth, 1558-1603*, published in 1959 as a volume in 'The Oxford History of England'. (Black also follows Charles Bayne in his brief account of Elizabeth's coronation and first parliament, citing his 1907 article as 'valuable'.) Geoffrey Elton draws on the book (without citation) in his widely read *England Under the Tudors* of 1955, while it is cited several times by Conyers Read in his *Mr Secretary Cecil and Queen Elizabeth* of the same year. But I have not found any references to Charles Bayne's book from the 1960s or later. In fact, his earliest article has proved his most durable Elizabethan work. Professor David Starkey identifies it as a principal source for Chapter 40, 'Coronation', of his book

Elizabeth: Apprenticeship, published in 2000, and cites it frequently in the notes to that chapter.

When Geoffrey Elton began his research under Professor John Neale in 1946 (according to the DNB) Professor Pollard was nearing the end of his life, 'releasing the reign of Henry VIII' to other scholars. Elton therefore told Neale that 'he'd do Henry VIII, sir.' He soon moved to Cambridge, where he became the 'most pungent and opinionated' lecturer at the university. Professor Elton's 'creative contribution to the subject and profession of history was greater than that of any of his peers and contemporaries', but he remained highly polemical, at one point pursuing a vendetta against Sir John Neale. In his book *The Tudor Revolution* of 1952 he vigorously expounded the view that England remained in the Middle Ages until the reforms of Henry VIII's reign, especially under Thomas Cromwell. That gave him a special perspective on Henry VII's reign and an interest in Charles Bayne's last book when it appeared in 1958.

Geoffrey Elton reviewed the book in volume lxxiv (1959) of the *English Historical Review* and his review (republished in *Studies in Tudor and Stuart Politics and Government*, volume I, in 1974) is worth analysing at length. He begins by noting 'this book has been a long time in the making' and criticising the way the legal texts are attached to it. 'Bayne's introduction', he says, 'bears all the marks of having been written in advance of the collection which it introduces.' He divides the book's contents into three parts: the operation of the Council, the Act of 1487 and the Council as court of Star Chamber. 'Only the second part of the introduction does work that need never be done again', he says. 'The discussion of the Act [of 1487] supersedes and in part nullifies all earlier writing on the subject.' On the Council as court, 'Bayne's analysis not only entirely replaces Leadam's but in such matters as procedure, competence and punishments provides some very welcome light'. Bayne contends that the Star Chamber was mainly a court for civil suits between private parties; 'much of this new view must certainly be accepted'.

So far the review is highly favourable. But polemic soon appears. Elton asserts that the Council as Star Chamber in fact dealt with every sort of crime, not mainly civil cases: 'To argue (as Bayne does) from the absence of evidence when only 194 cases survive from 24 years would seem dangerous in the extreme.' He admits that on the Council as a political body, 'Bayne has done a good deal to advance understanding'. But he attacks him fiercely for making a false distinction between Council and Star Chamber. This criticism hardly seems to be justified by the text of Bayne's book and may reflect Elton's obsession with the medieval quality of Henry VII's reign. He concludes: 'Important and sound as much of Bayne's work is, the basic flaw cannot be overlooked. The history of the early Tudor Council is still to be written and Bayne has not discharged the task for the reign of Henry VII. So much premised, it should be stressed that he has greatly contributed to this fascinating and exacting problem.'

Professor Elton returned to this theme in 1964 with an article for an Italian journal called 'Why the History of the Early Tudor Council Remains Unwritten' (also republished in *Studies in Tudor and Stuart Politics and Government*, volume I). At the outset he notes that there is no book on the early Tudor Council, despite its importance, and dismisses most early writings as inaccurate or misleading. The first works that Elton takes seriously are Pollard's articles from 1922: 'Pollard's virtues as a historian never shone more brightly than in this analysis of a complex problem.' He comments on some articles by Professor Dunham from 1943 and then on Charles Bayne's book, as follows:

'Between them Dunham and Bayne enormously advanced our understanding of the early-Tudor Council. Bayne mainly assisted in clarifying its work as a court. He ended the legend of a royal tribunal against trouble-makers and introduced us to a court for private persons' suits. He went some way towards sorting out the membership of Henry VII's Council and confirmed Dunham's chief and vital assertion (against Pollard) that there was a king's council, not just king's councillors.'

Elton then challenges various assumptions made by earlier authors. He attacks the views (attributed to Pollard) that a large council could not be a working council and that Henry VII's Council differentiated between councillors. He repeats his criticisms of Charles Bayne, asserting that there was no distinction between Council and court of Star Chamber and that, as a court, it dealt with crimes of all kinds. Finally, having reviewed the sources for writing the missing history of Henry VII's Council, he concludes: 'The state of the evidence is such that a truly well-based understanding will be hard to come by. Indeed, anyone who surveys this range of booby-trapped materials might well be tempted to retire and keep bees'. There is a strong impression that Elton contemplated undertaking such a work himself, but recoiled from it as too difficult.

Sir Geoffrey Elton lived on till 1994, but wrote no more on Henry VII's Council. The next important treatment is in *The Cardinal's Court* by John Guy, published in 1977. This book is mainly about the Star Chamber under Cardinal Wolsey, but the first chapter describes the court under Henry VII. Here Guy follows Charles Bayne in every detail, pointing out that his analysis is corroborated by later evidence discovered at the Public Record Office (where Guy was working). One passage deserves quoting at length:

'The work of Mr C. G. Bayne established that the litigation which came before Henry VII's Council in Star Chamber was primarily civil, though disguised as criminal, and between private parties. Even the Council's traditional jurisdiction in riot was largely set in motion by private bills and only very rarely by the government. Bayne's conclusions are broadly untarnished by the discovery that the arrangement of the misnamed

Star Chamber Proceedings, Henry VII at the PRO failed to include roughly one-third of the documents which survive for the reign. Although Bayne's total of 194 cases extant for the 24 years is thus invalidated, the real count being nearer 300, the proportional distribution of the suits between civil and criminal remains more or less constant. Of the suits not known to Bayne almost all began with the filing of a bill of complaint or petition by a private party.'

Guy concludes that no more than a tenth of the litigation before Henry VII's Council in Star Chamber was criminal in content, thus neatly exploding one of Sir Geoffrey Elton's main criticisms.

Though now 30 years old, Guy's book remains the latest authoritative account of the early Star Chamber, being cited, for example, in John A. Wagener's *Bosworth Field to Bloody Mary: An Encyclopaedia of the Early Tudors* of 2003. In his article 'The Great Council in the Reign of Henry VII', in the *English Historical Review*, volume ci (1986), Peter Holmes writes: 'Until further study is completed, discussion of Henry VII's Council pretty well begins and ends with the various scraps of evidence collected by late Tudor and early Stuart antiquaries and edited for the Selden Society by Bayne and Dunham'. As with his work on Elizabethan topics, Charles Bayne's account of Henry VII's Council has become accepted as the authentic version of events. Though he completed it as long ago as 1934, it still holds the field.

Conclusion

I have traced the impact of Charles Bayne's ICS career and his historical writings up to the present day. It remains to tie the two aspects of his work together and relate them to his life as a whole. At first sight there appears to be no link between his time in Burma and his later research on the Tudors. But in fact Bayne's ICS background strongly influenced his approach to historical studies. He writes the sort of history you would expect a bureaucrat to write. He keeps clear of broad overarching themes and avoids adventurous theories or sweeping conclusions. Instead he concentrates on the minute detail, building up his arguments from meticulous and wide-ranging research, only partly visible in his published work. In his article on Elizabeth's coronation, for example, he disposes of the underlying religious conflict in a few half-sentences, but the exact position of the queen's 'traverse' in Westminster abbey gets two full pages. In his early articles he focuses his formidable research powers on precise, limited questions. What did Elizabeth do at her coronation? Was her first parliament 'packed'? As his confidence grows, he becomes more ambitious in attempting full-length books on Elizabeth I's early diplomacy and Henry VII's Council. But he still prefers to stick to well-defined themes and keeps clear of open-ended issues with wide ramifications.

Charles Bayne had, to all appearances, a very successful career as a colonial administrator in Burma. He had many of the necessary qualities: a strong sense of duty; the ability to pick out the key issues from a mass of data; and the capacity to express himself fluently on paper. But as his career advanced, I believe that he found his responsibilities weighed heavily upon him. He was always more at ease with papers than with people. He was happy under a strong chief like Charles Crosthwaite, who left him in no doubt what was expected of him (even if he disagreed with it). He was likewise comfortable with his post of Revenue Secretary, with its well-defined obligations. But he was uneasy in the more visible and demanding position of Chief Secretary, with its open-ended responsibilities, under an unreliable chief like Frederic Fryer. He may also have had growing doubts about the wisdom of many of the policies being adopted in Burma.

He survived these pressures, at the cost of two breakdowns, thanks in large part, I am sure, to the support he got from Augusta. But once he had served his 25 years, he considered that he had discharged his duty to the ICS and to the puritan ethos he had inherited from his father. He decided to follow a different paternal example, devoting himself to research and writing. He was able to continue all those things he liked best in his ICS career, such as making sense of obscure and fragmentary data and setting out complicated arguments on paper. But he escaped all those he did not like, especially the burden of managing people, the need to follow instructions from others and the responsibilities of office, which preyed on his mind.

So he passed his long retirement working hard but doing what he enjoyed most, with the growing satisfaction of seeing his historical research in print and valued by the most noted scholars of his day. He passed through a difficult period in the late 1930s: he was over 75, Augusta's health was failing and he feared his last book might never find a publisher. But he was rescued by Professors Neale and Plucknett and was able to spend the last decade of his long life still hard at work. I have no doubt that the mental stimulus of his historical research contributed to his longevity.

This view of his life is not based on any direct evidence. But I am fortified in these conjectures because they match my own experience, two generations later. When I began researching my grandfather's life, I did not realise how closely his own career, both before and after retirement, would correspond with my own. His time in the ICS was much more arduous than mine in the Diplomatic Service. His published works will prove more durable than anything that I have written. Yet I feel able to say what he thought and felt, both because I am his grandson and because I have been through similar experiences myself.

Notes and References

Chapter 1. Ancestry, Birth and Education
The early history of the Baynes can be found in Alfred Lawrence, *The Clan Bain* (Inverness 1963), David Macdonald, *A History of Dingwall Parish Church* (Dingwall 1976) and Norman Macrae, *Dingwall's Thousand Years* (Dingwall 1923). The life of Peter Bayne (1830-1896) is recorded in the *Dictionary of National Biography,* Supplement Vol. I (1901); the entry was written by his elder son, the Rev Ronald Bayne. I have read Peter Bayne's *The Chief Actors in the Puritan Revolution,* a lively, partisan analysis of the Civil War in England and Scotland.

Charles Bayne's time at Uppingham is recorded in the School Roll, which shows Peter Bayne's address as Worcester Park. The information on ICS entry in this chapter is mainly taken from David Gilmour, *The Ruling Caste,* pages 29-68. Herbert Thirkell White likewise began his ICS career destined for another part of India, but was diverted to Burma before he reached his original posting – see *A Civil Servant in Burma,* page 16.

Chapter 2. In the Districts of Lower Burma
The most recent account of the early history of Burma and the first and second Burmese wars is in Thant Myint-U, *The River of Lost Footsteps* (2007); for earlier treatments, see Htin Aung, *A History of Burma* and John F. Cady, *A History of Modern Burma.* Thant Myint-U explains the kingdom of Burma's system of government in his scholarly work *The Making of Modern Burma* (2001).

Charles Bayne's early postings and qualifying exams are recorded in the *Histories of Service,* Burma, and the *Civil List* for Burma, 1881-1886. I have assumed that his experience in the districts outside Rangoon matched that of Herbert White, as recorded in *A Civil Servant in Burma,* pages 16-26, 36-44 and 95.

Copious information on Henzada and Myanaung is in the *Burma Gazetteer* for Henzada District, including river embankments, population growth, cholera and William Hall's role as settlement officer.

Comparable, though less detailed, material on Pyapon and Paungde is in the *Imperial Gazetteer of India*, Burma, volume I. The account of the land settlement process is from Sir George Scott's *Burma, a Handbook*, pages 153-8. George Hodgkinson's commendation of Charles Bayne is quoted from the *Report on the Revenue Administration of Burma* for 1884-5. Details on ICS leave entitlements are taken from *The Ruling Caste*, pages 273-277.

Herbert White gives a fairly idyllic picture of life in the districts, while George Grant Brown, in *Burma as I Saw It*, and Harold Fielding-Hall, in *The Soul of a People*, go much further. On Burmese women, see Gilmour, *The Ruling Caste*, pages 285-7. Kipling was much taken with them, when he visited Rangoon and Moulmein in 1889. His best-known evocation of Burma, 'Mandalay' from *Barrack-Room Ballads*, is, according to Gilmour, 'a poem of great charm and striking inaccuracy'. But his story 'Georgie Porgie', a Burmese version of 'Madam Butterfly' from *Life's Handicap*, has a more authentic ring.

Chapter 3.   The Secretariat in Peace and War
Herbert White, *A Civil Servant in Burma*, is a major source for life in the Secretariat at this time. The quotations are from pages 51-2, 90-95 and 207. A general account of the Ilbert Bill and its impact is in Gilmour, *The Ruling Caste*, pages 132-134.

A detailed analysis of Mindon's reforms, the growing confusion under Thibaw and the onset of the Third Burmese War is in Thant Myint-U, *The Making of Modern Burma*. Earlier accounts, from differing viewpoints, are in G. E. Harvey, 'The Conquest of Upper Burma', *Cambridge History of India*, volume 6; John F. Cady, *A History of Modern Burma*; and Htin Aung, *A History of Burma*. Lord Salisbury's role is described in Andrew Roberts, *Salisbury: Victorian Titan* (1999), pages 369-70. Eyewitness reports of the war and its aftermath are in Sir Charles Crosthwaite, *The Pacification of Burma* (quoted from page 7), Herbert White, *A Civil Servant in Burma* (quoted from pages 137 and 154-5) and Donald Smeaton, *The Loyal Karens of Burma* (quoted from page 4, while Vinton's letters are on pages 8-59).

The Kipling story mentioned is from *Plain Tales from the Hills* and the poem from *Departmental Ditties*. Other relevant works are 'A Conference of the Powers', from *Many Inventions*, and 'The Ballad of

Bo Dah Thone', from *Barrack-Room Ballads*. Kipling was prevented by his editor from going to Burma to cover the fighting. His only visit (see Notes to Chapter 2) was in 1889 on his way home from India – see Andrew Lycett, *Rudyard Kipling* (1999), pages 125, 156 and 173.

Chapter 4.   Pacifying Burma under Crosthwaite

Sir Charles Crosthwaite's private letters to Herbert White are pre-served in the Thirkell White papers in the British Library, Mss Eur/E254/1. They are more revealing than Crosthwaite's published account, *The Pacification of Burma*, which was written long after the event and does not mention Charles Bayne. It mainly deals with military operations, though pages 22-24 and 50-54 describe the reforms of village administration and pages 25, 95-99 and 128-132 cover military police. The White papers also contain letters from Sir Charles Bernard, E254/2.   White describes the Secretariat under Crosthwaite in *A Civil Servant in Burma*, pages 207-208 and 218-219. The quotations from Smeaton, *The Loyal Karens*, are from pages 3-4, 219-220 and 236.   For Frederic Fryer's diary, see the Notes to Chapter 5.

A detailed analysis of Crosthwaite's reforms is in Mya Sein, *The Administration of Burma*, especially pages 125-132 and 150-162. She also quotes, on page xxii, Herbert White's assessment of him. Thant Myint-U (*The Making of Modern Burma*, pages 210-8) concludes that Crosthwaite had little alternative to replacing the old administrative system, but there was plenty of contemporary criticism. Alleyne Ireland, *The Province of Burma*, pages 712-7, reproduces verbatim a minute by Crosthwaite from 1890 setting out his aims in local administration (see Notes to Chapters 7, 8 and 14).

Chapter 5.   Courtship, Marriage and Family

Much of the information in this chapter is taken from the Hodgkinson family trees and other papers collected by Percy Grieve, MP, the grandson of Margaret Elinor Hodgkinson; I am most grateful to his son, Dominic Grieve, MP, for giving me access to them. The Rev George Christopher Hodgkinson has a rather inaccurate entry in the DNB, volume V, page 65. His athletic feat was reported in the *Cambridge Advertiser*, 4 March 1840. George Band, *Summit: 150 Years of the Alpine Club* (2006) records

Hodgkinson as making the first ascent of the Aiguille Verte by the Moine ridge on 5 July 1865. His fellow climber Hudson would lose his life on the Matterhorn nine days later.

The Hodgkinson papers include a letter written by George James Hodgkinson from Hutwah after the wedding of his sister Bella in 1872, while further details of the husbands of Margaret Elinor and Esther Amy emerge from the *Bengal Directory* and *Thacker's Indian Directory*. George James Hodgkinson's obituary, including details of his funeral, appeared in the *Newark Advertiser* early in 1892, reprinted from a Rangoon newspaper.

Frederic Fryer's diaries are in the India Office collection in the British Library, Mss Eur/E355. Over his entire career he wrote 4-5 lines every day, often about his horses and the weather. He seldom mentions his work or offers comments on people, though social events and travels are noted. He records Esther Hodgkinson's wedding, but not Augusta's, though both appear in the marriage registers of Christchurch, the Rangoon cantonment church. Alice Bayne's baptism, however, is not found in any Burmese register.

Surviving Bayne family papers include Augusta's wedding photograph and a copy of her marriage settlement. After his marriage, Charles Bayne expected a year and nine months of furlough, but in fact he only got just over a year (compare Burma *Histories of Service* 1891 and 1892). Peter Bayne's third wife is mentioned, but not named in the DNB entry written by his elder son. Clotilda's marriage is noted in the *Biographical Note of Charles Latimer Marson* (dated 1933) that can be accessed on www.anglicanhistory.org.

Herbert White dedicates *A Civil Servant in Burma* to his wife Fanny, who shared his Burmese career of 32 years; they were married before coming to Burma. Burma's unhealthy reputation for European women, including Sir Alexander Mackenzie's experience recorded in the next chapter, is documented in *The Ruling Caste*, pages 285-7.

Chapter 6.   Revenue Secretary in the 1890s

Sir Frederic Fryer's diary (E355/32-8) is a principal source for this chapter. Sir Alexander Mackenzie's 'Note to my Locum Tenens' and correspondence with Lord Lansdowne are preserved in the White papers (E254/12). They do not reveal the exact date or cause of his first wife's death. The copious letters exchanged by both Mackenzie and Fryer with Lord Elgin are in the 9th Earl of Elgin's papers in the British Library (F84/66-73). Herbert White's account of life in the Secretariat under Mackenzie is from *A Civil Servant in Burma*, pages 256-8. His comments on Maymyo are from page 178 and on George Burgess from pages 18-19 and 277.

On the separation of ICS families, see Gilmour, *The Ruling Caste*, pages 301-6. Bayne family papers include the various photographs of Charles, Augusta, Alice and Ronald, while Hodgkinson papers include Emily Hodgkinson's will. I have visited the graves of Peter, Clotilda and Anna Bayne in Harlington churchyard and have on my bookshelves Kipling's *The Seven Seas* inscribed 'C.G.B. 9. 11. 96.'

Chapter 7. Managing Burma's Economy: Rice and Teak

As indicated in the text, Burma government documents are important sources for the first part of this chapter. A comprehensive review of early attempts at legislation on land alienation and tenancy is in the *Report of the Land and Agriculture Committee*, created by the new Burmese government in 1937, after the separation from India. Further background comes from Cady, *A History of Modern Burma*, pages 155-168 and Furnivall, *Colonial Policy and Practice*, pages 84-98 and 109-116.

On forests, the story emerges from the correspondence between Fryer and Lord Elgin in the Elgin papers, F84/72-73. There is useful background in Nisbet, *Burma under British Rule and Before*. Alleyne Ireland, *The Administration of Burma* (see notes to next chapter) reproduces, on page 654 onwards, the Burma Forest Act 1902. Burma's third source of wealth was oil, but there is no record of Charles Bayne's involvement with this.

Chapter 8. Unexpectedly Chief Secretary

The account of the Burmese Government at the start of this chapter is taken from Alleyne Ireland, *The Administration of Burma*, especially pages 117-120, which includes the quotation. Ireland was a professor from the University of Chicago who toured colonial territories in South-East Asia to gain ideas for the United States on how to administer the Philippines. He visited Burma some time between 1902 and 1904 and produced a very long report, more valuable for description than analysis.

The main sources for the narrative of the chapter are Sir Frederic Fryer's personal diaries and the manuscript letters he exchanged with Lord Curzon, E355/39-41 and 65-70. The letters mentioned from Bernard and Crosthwaite are in the Thirkell White papers, E254/1 and 2. Full details on Lord Curzon's reaction to the 'Rangoon outrage' are in Lord Ronaldshay, *The Life of Lord Curzon*, volume ii, pages 71-3, while David Gilmour has a shorter account in *Curzon*, page 172. The Parliamentary Questions are in Hansard for 12 June (column 896), 16 June (column 1335) and 22 June 1899 (column 266). Charles Bayne's abortive posting to Minbu is noted in *Histories of Service*, Burma.

For George Scott's career, see *Scott of the Shan Hills*, Scott's diaries edited by his widow, G. E. Mitten. The position on the Burma-China border, including the quotation from the Chief Secretary in 1902, is described in Woodman, *The Making of Burma*, pages 486-7.

Chapter 9.   The Departure of Smeaton and Fryer

Like the previous chapter, the main sources are Fryer's diary and his correspondence with Lord Curzon, E355/41-43 and 70-74. David Gilmour, *Curzon*, pages 156, 161 and 352n gives additional background, including Curzon's view of Fryer and Smeaton's vendetta.

Crosthwaite's letters to White are quoted from E254/1, while his and Mackenzie's views of Donald Smeaton are in Lord Elgin's papers, F84/64 and 66. George Scott's Durbar diaries are in *Scott of the Shan Hills*, pages 306-319.

Chapter 10.   Financial Commissioner and Leaving Burma

Sir Hugh Barnes' correspondence with Curzon and with his wife from Burma in 1903 is on microfilm in the British Library, IOR/pos/8603. The letters quoted from Crosthwaite and Fryer, as well as White's own letters to Curzon, are in the White papers, E254/1, 3 and 4. Fryer's letter of 5 February 1905 is the only evidence that Augusta stayed back in England after Charles' return to Burma in August 1904 (I found no reference in his diary).

Charles Bayne's activities as Financial Commissioner are documented in the *Reports of the Land Revenue Administration of Burma* for 1904-5 and 1905-6 and in his comments on five Settlement Reports from 1905, as described in the text. The papers on Bayne's contribution to Herbert White's Land Alienation Bill are in the India Office

Burma Proceedings, Revenue and Agriculture, for January-June 1906. The quotation from White, *A Civil Servant in Burma,* is from page 296. As in Chapter 8, further background is in the *Report of the Land and Agriculture Committee* of 1937, Cady, *History of Modern Burma,* pages 165-7 and Furnivall, *Colonial Policy and Practice,* pages 84-98.

The circumstances (though not the motivation) of Charles Bayne's departure from Burma are set out in India Office *Burma Home Proceedings (Appointments),* May 1906, and *Civil Leave and Deputation Allowances,* A to D, April 1905 to October 1907. The final tribute to Charles Bayne is from the Resolution introducing the Land Revenue Administration Report for 1905-1906, page 6. Herbert White uses a similar formula when first speaking of Charles Bayne in *A Civil Servant in Burma,* page 90.

Chapter 11.   Early Research: Queen Elizabeth I
The photographs mentioned in the first paragraph are in the Bayne papers. Otherwise, all this chapter is based on Charles Bayne's published works, as noted in the text and the Bibliography.

Chapter 12.   Family Life in Retirement
Crosthwaite's letters are in the Thirkell White papers, E254/1. Henry Stevenson's marriage to Alice Bayne is recorded in the Bengal Registers for 1910 and his career in the *India Office List.* Charles Bayne's role as examiner in Burmese is recalled in the letters about him gathered by Alan Gledhill in 1957 (see Notes to Chapter 13) and preserved in the Bayne papers. (In addition, these letters mention his job at the Ministry of Pensions.)

The Bayne papers also contain: Madge Bayne's vital photograph album; later photos showing Charles and Augusta with various grandchildren and at Ronald's wedding; family letters from 1939-1941; and Charles Bayne's will. The correspondence between Charles Bayne and Charles Newbold, of Hodgkinson and Beevor, is in the Hodgkinson papers.

Chapter 13.   Late Research: King Henry VII

Charles Bayne's last book is a major source for this chapter, including the Memoir written by Professor Plucknett. The letters gathered by Alan Gledhill for this memoir from those who remembered Bayne in Burma are preserved in the Bayne papers.

The assessments of Professor Albert Pollard and Professor Theodore Plucknett are taken from the *Oxford DNB* of 2004. Charles Bayne's correspondence with his academic colleagues about his last book (originals of incoming letters and drafts of outgoing ones) is in the Bayne papers. The correspondence continues after his death with my father Ronald Bayne, up to the final appearance of the volume in 1958.

Chapter 14.   Charles Bayne as Administrator and Historian

On colonial administration, Gilmour, *The Ruling Caste*, pages 210-28, comments on the quality of the ICS members in the Secretariat. Htin Aung is quoted from *The Stricken Peacock*, pages 95-6. Crosthwaite's minute is reproduced in Alleyne Ireland, *The Province of Burma*, pages 712-7. Further background on developments in Burma is in Furnivall, *Colonial Policy and Practice*, Robert Taylor, *The State in Burma*, Harvey, *British Rule in Burma* and Thant Myint-U, both *The Making of Modern Burma* and *The River of Lost Footsteps*.

On Tudor history, the assessments of Sir John Neale and Sir Geoffrey Elton are taken from the *Oxford DNB* of 2004. Otherwise this part of the chapter is based on the books and articles cited in the text and the Bibliography.

Bibliography

This bibliography covers books and other sources that are available in libraries. Some additional works appear in the Notes and References, which also cover private family papers. I have used the British Library India Office Collection and the libraries of Chatham House, the Institute of Historical Research, the London School of Economics and Political Science, the School of Oriental and African Studies and the Travellers Club and express my appreciation to their librarians.

Many of the quotations from these sources in the main text have been abbreviated by removing words and sentences, though always preserving the sense and spirit of the original passage. Words added to preserve the sense are shown in square brackets.

Published Works by Charles Bayne, his father Peter, and his brother Ronald

C. G. Bayne, 'The Coronation of Queen Elizabeth', *English Historical Review*, vol. xxii (1907), pp. 650-73 and vol. xxiv, (1909), pp. 322-3.

C. G. Bayne, 'The First House of Commons of Queen Elizabeth', *English Historical Review,* vol. xxiii (1908), pp. 455-476 and 643-82.

C. G. Bayne, 'The Visitation of the Province of Canterbury, 1559', *English Historical Review*, vol. xxviii (1913), pp. 636-77.

C. G. Bayne, *Anglo-Roman Relations* 1558-65, Oxford, the Clarendon Press, 1913.

C. G. Bayne and William H. Dunham, (editors), *Select Cases in the Council of Henry VII*, Selden Society Publications, vol. 75, 1958.

Peter Bayne, *The Chief Actors in the Puritan Revolution*, 1879.

Rev Ronald Bayne (editor), *Arden of Feversham*, London, J. M. Dent and Co, 1897.

Rev Ronald Bayne (editor), *The Life of Fisher*, transcribed from MS Harleian 6382, Early English Text Society, extra series no cxvii, 1921.

Manuscript Collections in the British Library

Sir Hugh Barnes' papers, MSS/Eur/Ior/pos/8603, microfilm:
  Correspondence with Lord Curzon and with his wife, 1903.
The 9th Earl of Elgin's papers, MSS/Eur/F84:
  Correspondence with Persons in India, 1894-1898,
  F84/64-73.
Sir Frederic Fryer's papers, MSS/Eur/E355:
  Diaries, 1888-1905, E355/28-45
  Correspondence with Lord Curzon, 1899-1903, E355/65-74.
Sir Herbert Thirkell White's papers, MSS/Eur/E254:
  Letters from Sir Charles Crosthwaite, E254/1.
  Letters from Sir Charles Bernard, E254/2.
  Letters from Sir Frederic Fryer, E254/3.
  Correspondence with Lord Curzon, E254/4.
  Papers related to Burmese Administration (includes
  correspondence between Lord Lansdowne and Sir
  Alexander Mackenzie), E254/12.
Registers of Baptisms, Marriages and Funerals, Bengal
  (includes Burma), 1890-1910: Microfilm, N/1/223, 261, 263,
  289 and 365.

Government Reports and Other Publications

Burma Home Proceedings (Appointments), 1906.
Burma Proceedings, Revenue and Agriculture, 1906.
Civil Leave and Deputation Allowances, A to D, 1905-7.
Civil List, Burma, 1881-1907.
Histories of Service, ICS Burma, 1881-1907.
Imperial Gazetteer of India, Burma, volume I, 1908.
India List, Civil and Military, 1881-1895
India Office List, 1895-1907.
W. S. Morrison, *Burma Gazetteer, Henzada District*, 1915.
Report on the Administration of Burma, 1890-1.
Report on Forest Administration in Burma, 1890-1 to 1897-8.
Report on the Revenue Administration of Burma, 1884-5, 1890-1 to
  1897-8.
Report on the Land Revenue Administration of Burma, 1904-5 and
  1905-1906.
Report of the Land and Agriculture Committee, 1937.

Books by Charles Bayne's Contemporaries in Burma

Sir Charles Crosthwaite, *The Pacification of Burma*, 1912, reissued 1968.

R. Fielding-Hall, *The Soul of a People*, 1898.

R. Grant Brown, *Burma as I Saw it, 1889-1917*, 1926.

Alleyne Ireland, *The Province of Burma*, Report for the University of Chicago, 1907.

G. E. Mitton (Lady Scott), *Scott of the Shan Hills*, 1936. This memoir incorporates Sir George Scott's diaries.

John Nisbet, *Burma under British Rule and Before*, 1901. Nisbet was a Forest Conservator in Burma.

Sir George Scott, *Burma: a Handbook*, 3rd Edition, 1921.

Donald Smeaton, *The Loyal Karens of Burma*, 1887.

Sir Herbert Thirkell White, *A Civil Servant in Burma*, 1913.

More Recent Works on Burma and the Indian Civil Service

John F. Cady, *A History of Modern Burma*, 1958. A very useful source, though slightly biased towards the American Baptist missionaries.

F. S. V. Donnison, *Public Administration in Burma*, 1953. Donnison served with the ICS in Burma, 1922-48, rising to Chief Secretary.

J. S. Furnivall, *Colonial Policy and Practice: a Comparative Study of Burma and Netherlands India*, 1948. Furnivall served with the ICS in Burma, 1902-25.

David Gilmour, *Curzon*, 1994.

David Gilmour, *The Ruling Caste: Imperial Lives in the Victorian Raj*, 2005. This is an invaluable source of information on the ICS.

G. E. Harvey, 'The Conquest of Upper Burma', *Cambridge History of India*, vol. 6, 1932, pp. 432-448. Harvey served with the ICS in Burma, 1912-34.

G. E. Harvey, *British Rule in Burma, 1824-1942*, 1946.

Htin Aung, *The Stricken Peacock: Anglo-Burmese Relations, 1752-1948*, 1965.

Htin Aung, *A History of Burma*, 1967.

Mya Sein, *The Administration of Burma*, 1938, reissued 1971.

Lord Ronaldshay, *The Life of Lord Curzon*, vol. ii, 1928.

A. J. Stockwell, 'Expansion in South-East Asia', *Oxford History of the British Empire*, vol. 3, 1999.

Robert H. Taylor, *The State in Burma*, 1987.

Thant Myint-U, *The Making of Modern Burma*, 2001. A very thorough, scholarly analysis of the kingdom of Burma in the 19th century.

Thant Myint-U, *The River of Lost Footsteps*, 2007. A more discursive treatment of Burma from the earliest times up to the present.

Dorothy Woodman, *The Making of Burma*, 1962.

Philip Woodruff, *The Men Who Ruled India: the Guardians*, 1954.

Works on Tudor History

J. B. Black, *The Reign of Elizabeth, 1558-1603*, 1959.

G. R. Elton, *England under the Tudors*, 1955.

G. R. Elton, 'Henry VII's Council' and 'Why the History of the Early Tudor Council Remains Unwritten', *Studies in Tudor and Stuart History and Politics*, vol. 1, 1974, pp. 294-300 and 308-338.

J. A. Guy, *The Cardinal's Court*, 1977.

P. J. Holmes, 'The Great Council in the Reign of Henry VII', *English Historical Review*, vol. ci (1986), pp. 840f.

I. S. Leadam, *Select Cases before the King's Council and the Star Chamber*, 1477-1509, Selden Society Publications vol. 16, 1903.

J. E. Neale, *The Elizabethan House of Commons*, 1949.

J. E. Neale, *Elizabeth and Her Parliaments*, 2 volumes, 1953.

J. E. Neale, 'The Biographical Approach to History', *Essays in Elizabethan History*, 1958.

A. F. Pollard, 'The Coronation of Queen Elizabeth', *English Historical Review*, vol. xxv (1910), pp. 125-6.

A. F. Pollard, *The Reign of Henry VII from Contemporary Sources*, 3 volumes, 1914.

A. F. Pollard, *The History of England from the Accession of Edward VI to the Death of Elizabeth (1547-1603)*, 1919.

A. F. Pollard, 'The Council, Star Chamber and Privy Council', *English Historical Review*, vol. xxxvii (1922), pp. 357f. and 516f. and vol. xxxviii (1923), pp. 42f.

Conyers Read, *Mr Secretary Cecil and Queen Elizabeth*, 1955.

David Starkey, *Elizabeth: Apprenticeship*, 2000.

J. A. Wagener, *From Bosworth Field to Bloody Mary: an Encyclopaedia of the Early Tudors*, 2003.